2 Oriole Drive
Woodstock, NY 12498
Phone 845.679.2188
845.684.2150
www.cslewispublicity.com
david@cslewispublicity.com

David C. Lewis, Vice President

ONE DROP OF POISON
How One Bad Leader Can Slowly Kill Your Company

SEAN LEMSON, ACC, CPCC

S LEMSON PUBLISHING

S Lemson Publishing

Copyright © 2024 by Sean Lemson

All rights reserved, including the right to reproduce this book or portions thereof in any form whatsoever.

First edition March 2024

To inquire about guest speaking engagements or consulting, please contact sean@motivatedoutcomes.com.

Manufactured in the United States of America

Cover Design: DiztriX
Photography: Hrach Hovhannisyan

ISBN 978-1-7330042-3-7
ISBN 978-1-7330042-4-4 (e-book)

Dedication

This book is dedicated to all the leaders I've had over the years. Like many of us, I have experienced leadership that ranged from terrible to awe-inspiring and everything in between. The greatest leaders inspired and encouraged me to grow. The worst taught me how urgently this book needed to be written.

Acknowledgments

Many people have shaped the message you're about to read. I would like to thank several mentors for inspiring me.

Bernie Clark is a genuinely wonderful human being who always saw more in me than I saw in myself. He taught me, never shamed me for not knowing, and created the safety for me to fail. I did the work, but he is the one who called me forth and I will always be forever grateful for his guidance and his unshakable faith in me.

Patrick Goonan, a friend, a coach, a mentor, a teacher, a learner, and one who will forever be known to me as the person who picked me up from one of my darkest days, when I was covered with proverbial poison, and set me on my feet again. Words cannot express the gratitude I have for Pat.

Bob Posukonis is a leader who should be in the dictionary as exhibit A of servant leadership. Bob was one of the first leaders to empower me to try new approaches and, when those approaches were successful, we learned from each other, and he became an advocate for me and my methods. Without his political air cover and encouragement, I honestly don't think I'd be where I am today. He took many hits from a dysfunctional organization around us but *always* protected our team and did what was right for the company—even if they didn't acknowledge it. Bob remains a friend today and one whose guidance I seek out and deeply appreciate.

To those who helped me hone this book by reading early copies: Becky Farone, Sonja Figueroa, Ron Forrester, Bob Posukonis, Joel Riddle, Natalie Solomon, and Monique Verheul. Thank you. The book is immeasurably better because of your feedback.

Finally, to my editing team at Warner Coaching, a warm thank you. If you think you have a firm grasp of the English language, a good editor will liberate you from that belief very quickly. I have a good editing team and I am forever humbled by their eagle eyes. Any mistakes that remain are my own.

Contents

FOREWORD I

INTRODUCTION
    We Don't Value the Same Things vi
    The Intended Audience xi
    Basic Layout of the Book xii
    Deeper Dives and Other Resources xiii
    My Writing Style xiv

PART ONE: TOXICITY

CHAPTER 1: TOXIC LEADERSHIP 3
    Bad Leadership Is a Virus 4
    Bad Leadership Is a Habit 6
    Toxic Leadership Archetypes 7
    When Things Get Clinical 18

CHAPTER 2: TOXIC CULTURES 23
    A Symphony of Bad Motives 24
    Easy to Build, Difficult to Destroy 26
    Toxic Culture Ingredients 27
    The Toxic Soup Recipe 38

CHAPTER 3: THE ILLUSION OF UNDERSTANDING 41
    Goodhart's Law 42
    Measuring What Matters 46
    Measuring Frequency 47
    Engagement Surveys 48
    Metrics Fixation 50

CHAPTER 4: THE ILLUSION OF CONTROL 53
    The Cynefin Framework 54
    Budgeting and the Illusion of Control 57
    The Role of Trust 57

CHAPTER 5: TOXIC COMMUNICATION 59
    Actions Matter 60
    Credibility: Your Most Important Tool 63

PART 2: THE COST OF BAD LEADERSHIP

CHAPTER 6: HIGH TURNOVER — 67
- A Leadership Problem — 68
- Turnover Is Expensive — 70
- Why Companies Ignore Turnover — 72
- Reputation Loss — 76

CHAPTER 7: LOSS OF INNOVATION — 79
- Five Ways to Lose Your Innovation Edge — 80
- Calculating the Cost — 86

CHAPTER 8: LOSS OF AGILITY — 89
- Contributing to Churn — 91
- Avoiding Accountability — 92
- Kissing Up and Hitting Down — 93
- Distrusting Employees — 94
- Death Marches — 94

CHAPTER 9: TAKING POISON HOME — 97
- The Health Connection — 99
- The Healthcare Connection — 101
- The Societal Connection — 102

PART 3: BECOMING A BETTER LEADER

CHAPTER 10: YOUR MINDSET ABOUT LEADERSHIP — 109
- Motives: A Mindset in Practice — 114
- A Beginner's Mind — 117
- Empathy Is Required — 125

CHAPTER 11: YOUR MINDSET ABOUT THE WORK — 129
- Effectiveness over Efficiency — 130
- Outcomes over Outputs — 131
- Complex vs. Complicated — 132
- Growth vs. Fixed Mindset — 133
- Trust and Organizational Health — 136
- Less Is More — 141
- Leadership Stances — 142

CHAPTER 12: SUCCESSFUL LEADERSHIP BEHAVIORS — 147
- The Gardner vs. The Chess Player — 149
- Create Effective Organizations — 151

Lead Ethically	157
Connect People with Meaning	159
Coach, Don't Play	162

CHAPTER 13: A CREATOR AND DESTROYER OF WORLDS — 167

Create Stability	168
Create Safety	172
Create Connection	176
Create Clarity	178
Create Purpose	179
Create Impact	181

CHAPTER 14: TOXIC LEADERSHIP ARCHETYPES REVISITED — 185

The Chess Master	187
The Peacock and The Ladder Climber	189
The Micromanager	193
The Invertebrate	195
The Drill Sergeant	198
The Data Freak	200
The Bottom Liner	201
The Squirrel	203
The Graveyard Whistler	206
The Value of Coaching and Therapy	208

PART 4: BECOMING A BETTER COMPANY

Incentives	212

CHAPTER 15: HUMAN RESOURCES — 215

Reimagining Human Resources	217
Disconnection from Policy Impact	220
Contractors: A Class System	222

CHAPTER 16: FINANCE — 225

The Distant King	226

CHAPTER 17: SAVING STARFISH — 231

APPENDIX A: YOUR MINDSET ABOUT LEADERSHIP — 237

Mindset Exercise	238

APPENDIX B: THE TWENTY-FIRST CENTURY LEADERSHIP MANIFESTO — 239

ONE DROP OF POISON

Foreword

Having been an engineer all my life, obviously I love technology. But it wasn't until I became a leader in technology that I learned the most important lesson of my career: technology is the easy part; people are the hard part. I would venture to guess that this is true for any leader in any line of work.

This isn't to say that people mean to be difficult or cause problems. They generally don't. But enabling teams of people to work together effectively and efficiently can be extraordinarily difficult. Far more difficult than any technical (or other) project. Each person on a team brings a different background, different perspectives, and different aspirations. This is what makes teams so strong. It is also why it takes a bit of magic (dare I say, leadership) to get everyone aligned to the ultimate goal.

And so it was, as this new leadership idea was dawning on me, that I met Sean. I was leading an engineering organization, which consisted of over two dozen teams. For the most part, my teams were working well internally as well as with other teams. However, there were a handful of teams that just didn't seem to be clicking and I wanted to get them help.

I had heard of Sean's work in other parts of the organization and asked to meet with him to see if he could help. I remember one of the first things he asked me when we met: "Ron, what is one thing all leaders have?" I smiled because this one was easy, or so I thought. *One thing?* I thought. *I can name a bunch.* I rattled off all of the qualities of not just good, but great leaders: empathy, empowerment, transparency, integrity, vulnerability. I could have kept going, but Sean gently stopped me and said, "No, it's none of those things. It's followers. A leader is simply someone who has people following them."

Sean started with this question because he wanted me to understand that I was a leader. I had people following me. Upon establishing that fact, he talked to me about how leadership had a multiplying impact, good or bad, on how teams worked together. He mentioned that he always likes to start coaching at the leadership level because, regardless of how talented the people are in an organization, leaders can quickly ruin any chance that teams have of becoming great teams. I wanted to lead great teams.

From that moment on, Sean became a truth-teller for me. I would seek his counsel often and we worked together to solve some of the many issues that arose when trying to get 150 people to work toward the same goals. Sometimes he would tell me things I didn't like to hear. But they were truths nonetheless, and I am better because of them. On one occasion, he told me that some tried-and-true metrics I expected the teams to improve would, indeed, improve. But if we focused on them without first considering the dynamics of the humans on the team, even more important metrics, such as quality and engagement, would suffer. He was holding me accountable as a leader in a way that taught me how to be a better one. He taught me to think beyond management. Yes, I could manage the numbers, but would people stop following me in the process? Wouldn't that be a bigger problem in the end?

Once Sean oriented me and my leaders to think beyond our numbers and into the way our behaviors impacted our teams, he said he would embed in each of the struggling teams for two weeks, or a month at most, and in the end have them running like clockwork. This wasn't hubris. It was his experience. He knew that with leaders focused on the right things, with the right expectations, these teams would do great things. Word got around. Soon, my teams were requesting Sean's help at the first sign of struggle. The teams themselves wanted to improve. They *wanted* to be great! Not just because I wanted them to, but because *they* wanted to.

Sean's title was classified as an individual contributor. If you looked him up in our HR system, it would say nothing about him being a leader. But I followed him. Many people followed him. We followed him because he told us the truth, and he clearly cared about us and our teams. He was and is a walking example of how he began our relationship: He is a leader because people follow him.

You, the reader, are fortunate to have this book in your hands. You will read things that make perfect sense to you, and you will read some things that you may not want to admit are true about the way you lead. Pay particular attention to the latter if you want to look behind you and realize that, regardless of your title, you too are a leader because others are following you.

Ron Forrester
CTO, TaskRabbit
February 2024

INTRODUCTION

I was nervous and excited. In just a few minutes, I'd be meeting my boss's new boss, Barbara. She was hired to fill a new position to head up program management in our part of the company. Our team of coaches was responsible for helping teams adopt Agile. Agile is a methodology that is aimed at helping teams create value for customers faster while helping companies pivot quicker to changing competitive environments. We had been struggling to have the impact we knew we could be having. We just couldn't get traction at the senior leadership level, and having a senior director with Agile chops would help.

So, there we were, my peers and I, waiting to meet Barbara for the first time. She hadn't officially started yet but agreed to meet with us for lunch. We were looking forward to swapping a few stories and getting to know each other. Little did we know, there would be none of that.

From nearly the first five minutes of knowing us, Barbara jumped in with sentences starting with, "What I'll be expecting from you . . ." or "What I'll be looking for from you is . . ." usually followed by something obvious we'd tried to do unsuccessfully because we kept running into these political barriers. *Is she even listening?* I thought. We were all transformation experts. We knew what was stopping the company from transforming, and it was none of the things she was expecting us to do.

Her all-exclamation-points-and-no-question-marks style was a big red flag for us. It told us that she viewed us as inexperienced and in need of her instructions rather than her support. We told our boss that we were getting a weird vibe and he agreed it wasn't looking right, but he said, "Maybe she just comes in a bit hot to new jobs." We'd let her settle in and give it another try later.

Fast forward several weeks later, my boss set up another meeting with Barbara and us. I knew that vulnerability was important in trust building, so I went in willing to discuss the places we were failing and where we saw opportunities for her to help. We were a small team of four who was single-handedly trying to transform a deeply matrixed and political organization of nearly fifteen hundred people and almost two hundred teams. We suspected that she was still getting her head around the size of the task ahead of her and would appreciate inside information from four frontline senior folks, so we tried to help her get acclimated to the deep organization and political history.

During the meeting, we explained that, when it would have helped the most, leaders in the company were setting Agile aside. We were having great success with teams, but the portfolio layer was resistant and stuck between Agile teams and an executive team with a waterfall mentality (if you're an Agile coach reading this, I know you'll need urgent care for your eyes being rolled so far back in your skull).

After listening to us for about fifteen minutes, she finally said, "You're all directors, right?" Technically that was true; even though we didn't have direct reports, we were at a director pay grade.

"Yes," we replied.

"Well, these are the kinds of problems I'm paying you to solve," she said.

And with that, the meeting was basically over. Not physically, of course. We were in the room for another fifteen minutes, but I can't recall what was said after that. I was just lost in my thoughts trying to come to grips with the fact that we now had a skip-level boss with zero leadership skills. With Barbara in charge, our problems were going to get worse, not better.

We Don't Value the Same Things

Several months after the infamous "these are the problems I'm paying you to solve" meeting, Barbara was starting to get itchy to show some results to her leadership team. She began asking the teams to put together a dog and pony show[1] called a Quarterly Business Review (QBR). She tasked my boss with putting it together each quarter. This entailed polling the 160 people in Barbara's organization to ask them for "wins." Once the wins started coming in, then the real work began. Hours and hours of punctuation, editing, massaging data, and finalizing into a Keynote deck. The process was so time-consuming and laborious (read: expensive) that we often started the next quarter's QBR deck almost immediately after the current quarter's was presented.

Years earlier in my consulting practice, I had developed a highly effective training program of individual psychology, team psychology, team dynamics, and process followed by team coaching and, if needed, coaching with individual managers and team members. It had turned some of our company's most dysfunctional teams around and had earned such a reputation for itself that some of my colleagues now jokingly referred to me as the Team Whisperer.

I had recently wrapped up a large team engagement using my training program. I had reorganized a team of fifteen infighting engineers, all focused on different missions, into three squads all pulling work from a single backlog. It was a massive improvement in almost every regard. The managers and the teams were happier and working more efficiently, and the company benefitted from a much more resilient, adaptable force of motivated employees. So, when my boss suggested that I present this work as the kind of win Barbara was asking for, I readily agreed, as I was quite proud of the outcome.

I collected testimony from the leaders of the team, presented engagement scores, and described in bullet form the many benefits the team was now enjoying in their new formation. I thought the work essentially spoke for itself.

---

[1] Most of my experience with QBRs have been negative because many company cultures are toxic. However, they can be very useful if the leaders who attend them are free of toxicity. If your company's culture is overly focused on performers and you have a large population of ladder-climber leaders, the QBR is the main event where much of this dysfunction gets a spotlight.

I knew I was in trouble when my boss sent me a Slack message that said, "Barbara wants to meet with us about your win." It seems we were destined to get more of her direction.

"These are nice, Sean," she said, "but I need to see some numbers. Give me . . . um . . . three numbers." Because this was essentially a new team now, there were no performance baselines we could take that wouldn't feel faked, but we did have loads of qualitative data about team morale, trust, and engagement improvements. When I presented those, Barbara was not impressed. She wanted to see quantitative data about a qualitative improvement (we'll talk more about data later). I didn't have it, so she pulled my win from the deck. With that action, I watched everything I saw as the value I added to this company be tossed out with it.

I wish I could tell you that I recovered from that, but I never did. My own engagement fell like a rock. And looking around the organization, I noticed that I wasn't alone. In the nearly three years I worked under Barbara, the engagement scores of the 160 people in our organization became and stayed terrible. Barbara's boss and the HR group at the company didn't seem to care. We went from a vibrant, entrepreneurial, growth-oriented, innovative workforce to a zombie-like, mumbling-under-our-breaths, dispirited group scared for our jobs. In conversation after conversation, many of us were individually being told that what we were bringing wasn't valuable to her. We saw our leaders, who spoke up on our behalf, being demoted and punished because Barbara viewed disagreement as disloyalty. Safety disappeared virtually overnight. And most of us took our stress and anxiety home with us daily.

In this way, Barbara negatively affected over a hundred employees and their families for years. In the end, she ended up laying off nearly a third of the people in the organization. These were high-performing people who loved the company. Their lives were all upended.

As you were reading about Barbara, odds are good that you were recalling your own experience with a bad leader. Maybe you work for someone like Barbara right now. Bad leaders are a very common problem. Time and time again, poisonous leaders get into their roles without the right skills or motives. This happens even though the knowledge of how to be a good leader isn't exactly a secret. If you do a search in your favorite book catalog for "leadership," you'll find tens of thousands of results. Leadership is not a fresh topic to write about, yet its topical popularity is also its downside. Everyone seems to have authored an opinion about it (including some terrible leaders). Not only is the market flooded with advice that ranges from amazing to terrible, it's also just flooded!

Before writing this book, I deeply immersed myself in over forty books on leadership. Some of them so accurately described the dearth of good leadership in companies in the face of an uncertain world, I thought for sure they were written within the past twelve months. Time and time again, I'd refer to the copyright dates and discover that many were written a decade or two ago . . . even six decades ago in one case!

Solid, research-backed advice about leadership has been available for a long time. In fact, never in the history of mankind have we known more about how to cultivate human creativity, what motivates and demotivates workers, how people want to be treated (at work and home), how teams become high performing or dysfunctional, and how companies become innovative or disappear. So why do leaders like Barbara continue to be hired and promoted? Why can't we seem to get this right in our companies?

I believe these anti-patterns[2] of leadership continue to flourish for four reasons:

---

[2] I like Wikipedia's definition of an anti-pattern as a common response to a recurring problem that is usually ineffective and risks being highly counterproductive. Anti-patterns nearly always initially appear to be effective and appropriate, but they have more bad consequences than good. Also, a more effective solution usually already exists but is being ignored. I can't think of a more appropriate word to describe the state of leadership today.

1. **Leadership tactics seem like they're working when they're not.** Like all anti-patterns, they look good on the surface but often show short-term results at the expense of long-term company and employee health. Many companies promote individuals who demonstrate short-term results into leadership positions; they are often not measuring the right things, so they don't see the data screaming that their environment is toxic.

2. **External pressure.** There are external forces that incentivize companies to pursue short-term wins over long-term health, e.g., layoffs, offshoring, and low wages to meet quarterly and annual earnings targets (with the associated bonuses for meeting them), industry analysts pressuring executives for short-term returns, etc. The short-term outcome is severely disconnected from the long-term health of the company and its workforce. Authoritarian leaders who lack empathy thrive in these environments.

3. **The alternative seems too "touchy feely."** Being a good leader is more about *who you are* than *what you do*. It's more about psychology and less about process. It's more about how you treat others than how much you know about what those others are doing. It's more about your motives for being a leader than your technical chops. Not everyone is cut from that cloth. Showing up in a way that gets employees to *be* a certain way is much more difficult than getting them to *do* a certain thing. It requires a completely different set of skills. Companies that prioritize profits over their employees hire and promote cutthroat leaders who use people like resources in the name of the companies' success.

4. **The benefit is fast, the damage is slow.** It's easy for companies to be lulled into thinking leadership is doing things right if profits are increasing. The kind of damage that anti-patterns of leadership create—becoming harder and more expensive to find talented employees, declining

innovation, the company's reputation growing as a bad place to work—is insidious and slow. So slow that it's often difficult to connect it to leadership at all—especially in medium to large companies.

I wrote this book because I feel that what is needed is the careful exploration of *why* so many leaders are poisonous and how that poison can slowly kill a company. I also want to help leaders to ensure they're not unintentionally poisoning their teams like Barbara did.

Some of the concepts in this book are unabashedly not new. As I mentioned, some go as far back as the mid-twentieth century. It's not good enough for me to put yet another book into the catalog on the topic that goes over the same old material. We must cover some of that material because, well, the problems of poor leadership are still present, and the advice remains much the same. My hope is that I've blended my own wisdom with the works of those whose shoulders I'm standing on to present a more complete picture of toxic leadership. Bad leadership is a slow, interconnected dance between anti-patterns, bad policies, and the mindsets of the people involved . . . the individuals drawn to power and the systems that reward them. It's the disconnected policies from human resources and finance departments and the incentives that drive those misguided policies.

The Intended Audience

Unless you're the owner of your company, you have a leader. Even CEOs have leaders. The only thing that changes with the level of leader you are is the number of people who are impacted, negatively or positively, by your leadership.

Working for a toxic leader at some point in one's career is nearly universal, so I think most people will find this book useful, but I wrote it for three distinct audiences who need to hear the same message for different reasons:

1. **Leaders** of all levels of experience, many of whom are unintentionally and unwittingly doing it wrong and need

to spot their own behaviors to change them before it poisons their teams and/or organization.

2. **Employees who are impacted** by poor leadership and are looking for the right words to push for change, and/or who need help spotting both good and bad leadership at their companies or at companies they're considering working for. Change of this magnitude doesn't just come from those who need to change, it also requires others to demand that change. My hope is that this book gives words to those most impacted so they can call for the change they deserve.

3. **HR and finance** create policies that, most often unintentionally, drive some of the worst leadership behavior we see today. I frequently coach leaders who tell me, "I have to do this because HR tells me to," or "I can't do the right thing because HR/finance won't let me." When policies are driving poor leadership, they're working *against* the company while ostensibly trying to work for it. We'll continue to come back to these wise words in different contexts: Bad incentives can make good people do bad things. Many of the policies that cause leaders to be toxic are rooted in bad incentives created by HR and finance executives who in turn are facing bad incentives from outside the company.

Basic Layout of the Book

In Part One, we'll explore what we mean by toxic leadership. We'll define the poisonous leadership anti-patterns and how some leaders inadvertently dig themselves into a hole when they communicate to their employees. Then we'll face the hard truth that most leaders today are delusional about how much they understand and how much control they have. We'll wrap up with a look at how all this ties together into a toxic culture.

In Part Two, we'll look at the costs of getting this wrong: the actual financial costs that are buried or disguised in your profit and loss statement and some that, most insidiously, don't show up there but are very real nonetheless.

In Part Three, we'll look at what leaders of all levels can do to improve their corners of the world—whether that's a small team of individuals or an entire enterprise. The focus will be personal: what you, as a new or veteran leader, can do differently to contribute to a less toxic environment. We'll look at that overused and misunderstood term "servant leadership" and learn about the elusive "high performing team" and your role as a leader in growing one.

No matter what level you are at a company, you're likely going to run into some institutional root causes for toxicity. Everything from the structure and purpose of various divisions and departments to the incentives of company policies. In Part Four, we'll cover how these structures and incentives not only weaken the walls of defense against toxicity but can even be the cause of it. We will explore how companies can shift their organizations to root out the poison. This includes retasking HR and finance to create the kinds of policies and processes that make the company culture healthier, improve employee engagement, and increase innovation. Of course, the larger the company, the longer and more effort these kinds of changes will take.

Deeper Dives and Other Resources

There is a significant body of research written by many well-known thought leaders in the field of leadership and psychology. We all benefit from their words. Throughout the book, watch for the sections labeled ***Deeper Dive***, where I point you to authors who have explored in more depth the topic at hand. In this way, you can follow the rabbit down the hole on any topic that deeply resonates with you. You will find this list of deeper dive resources on my company's website motivatedoutcomes.com, including those I discover after the book goes to press. There is also a YouTube channel for Motivated Outcomes with videos on the concepts contained in the book and much more about the art and science of leadership and team performance. This is an ongoing project, so keep an eye on the channel for new content and dare I say, "like and subscribe!"

My Writing Style

I think it would be good for me to alert you to my writing style and approach to the topic of leadership. I'm not writing a dry dissertation about how the X axis intersects with the Y to illustrate the . . . (yawn). I'm trying to change mindsets and behaviors. Because human beings are complex creatures, many concepts will appear in one place and then reappear in different contexts later on. I don't want you to have to determine how the concepts apply in these changing contexts, so I'm going to keep bringing them up throughout the book. The repetition is by design. There should be no reason for you to have to connect the dots because I'm going to paint the pictures as thoroughly as I can.

My style can be blunt at times. It's not that I don't want to be your friend, it's just that I'm that friend who cares so much that he's willing to cut through the crap with you. If there was ever a topic that is ready for some in-your-face talk, it's leadership. We simply cannot afford to beat around the bush as a society any longer and, as you'll see, you cannot afford to do that at your company either. In these pages, we're going to face some of these hard truths together. But I'm also going to try to inject some humor along the way because why shouldn't we face the harsh reality with a little self-deprecating laughter?

Whether you're the CEO of a Fortune 500 company, a mid-level leader, or are just aspiring to become a leader, I hope you will benefit from a new awareness of your own leadership and its impact after reading this book. It represents nearly two decades of training, experience, and observation as a professional coach. Not only have I advised leaders, but I've also worked for many of them. I've seen it done well and I've seen it done so poorly that when you read about them in these pages, you'll think I'm making up the stories (only names have been changed). I've been to therapists and suffered physical health problems as the result of toxic leadership, and I've been launched to heights I never believed I could reach by good leaders. This broad range of experiences at the hands of others has led me to a meaningful understanding of the power and responsibility of leadership, not just in our companies but in our politics, our personal lives, our parenting, and our religious and educational institutions.

Toxic leaders can bring out the worst in us. They can make us toxic to our friends and loved ones. They can jeopardize our health and, collectively, the health of society. But leaders can also create an environment where people can flourish and get deep gratification from their work, where toxicity is rooted out and guarded against for the good of everyone—including the company itself.

If you are a leader, the power is in your hands. I come to you in this book as an unrelenting spokesperson for the frustrated workers in your company who might even report to you . . . the ones waiting for you to get it together as a leader so they can stop jumping from company to company. When they stay, you can finally benefit from their true creativity and dedication. Shall we open this door labeled "Better Leadership and Better Companies" and walk through together?

Our first stop is unpleasant but necessary. Let's get started.

PART ONE

TOXICITY

When a workplace becomes toxic, its poison spreads beyond its walls and into the lives of its workers and their families.

— Gary Chapman, author of *Rising Above a Toxic Workplace: Taking Care of Yourself in an Unhealthy Environment*

Chapter 1: Toxic Leadership

There's no such thing as an underperforming team, only underperforming leaders. Look for the problem in concentric circles around your desk.

– Matt Whiat, Founder, Chapman & Co. Leadership Institute

Bad Leadership Is a Virus

> *A Players hire A Players, but B Players hire C Players and C Players hire D Players. It doesn't take long to get to Z Players. The trickle-down effect causes bozo explosions in companies.*
> *– Steve Jobs*

Steve Jobs's leadership philosophy has this belief threaded through its entirety—for better or for worse: A Players love working with—and are not threatened by—other A Players. What they can't stand is working with B and C Players. While Jobs wasn't referring to leaders specifically, this quote was one of my first introductions to the idea that bad leadership spreads bad leadership.

Good leaders are not threatened by people who know more than they do. They don't have an ego constantly nagging at them that they're not good enough. They see it as their job to recruit the best, most talented people available. They then focus on providing an environment where those people can use their talents for the company's benefit. If good leaders have B Players on their teams, they work to get them performing like A Players. These leaders may have the skills to do the work their direct reports do, but they let their employees do their jobs and instead focus on honing their *leadership* skills.

Poisonous leaders, on the other hand, are quite threatened by other people's skills. It's not that they don't hire A Players, it's that they don't usually *like* their A Players after hiring them (and the feeling is often mutual). These leaders get their self-worth from having the answers, not from cultivating and nurturing teams of people who have those answers. A Players usually leave these toxic leaders at some point because the only thing an A Player dislikes more than working *with* a B Player is working *for* a B Player.

Put one B Player into a leadership role and look at how quickly you can have Steve Jobs's "bozo explosion." Allow or promote just one B Player to a position with hire/fire ability and your A Players will bail—and likely spread the word that your company isn't a good place to work. Over time, this will turn your organization into an organism that actively repels A Players and organically retains and promotes the rest of the alphabet.

I settled on the title for this book early on. As I told others about it, they would often tell me about an experience where they were happy at their company, loved their boss, and felt a real sense of loyalty to the company. Then it happened. Their boss left for a better opportunity and was replaced by a toxic leader who immediately brought in all his or her cronies, took everyone off their mission, and made it a terrible place to work. After hearing some form of this story so many times over the years, I've become convinced that many companies are rewarding the wrong behaviors and punishing the right ones.

Saying that bad leadership is a virus is not an understatement. It spreads just like one. The problem is that most bad leaders don't know they're bad at it.

Super Chickens[3]

I mentioned that Steve Jobs's A and B Player model was his operating belief, for better or worse. While I find the model useful to label leaders who are or aren't run by their egos, or to understand how bad leaders seem to replicate in many organizations, its utility ends there for me. Let me tell you when a fixation on A Players can go off the rails and turn toxic.

In the 1990s, Purdue University researcher William Muir conducted an experiment on chickens to try to increase their productivity (number of eggs laid). Muir continually selected for breeding only the most productive chickens for six generations[4]. At the end of the experiment, all but three of the "super chickens" were dead. They'd pecked the rest to death. The individually productive chickens had only achieved their

---

[3] I first learned about the super chicken concept from a TED talk given by Margaret Heffernan. Watch it yourself: https://www.youtube.com/watch?v=Vyn_xLrtZaY

[4] This is similar to the terrible leadership practice that Jack Welch, former CEO of General Electric, instilled of culling your bottom 10 percent of performers. A practice still happening at Amazon today with almost laughable results, as we'll discuss a bit later.

astounding results by suppressing the productivity of the rest. And so it is at companies that can become too obsessive about A Players. A culture that rewards ladder climbers and peacocks (we'll be discussing these archetypes shortly) makes everyone either a climber or a rung. Corporate Hunger Games, what fun. It's a fantastic way to accidentally create a toxic culture for all the right reasons.

Bad Leadership Is a Habit

Bad leadership spreads through hiring and promotion, but it also spreads through example and culture. Bad leaders cause others to raise their defenses and become less cooperative. After this has been going on for some time, it becomes "the way things are done here" or "that's just the [insert company/team name] culture." In these environments, even leaders who are usually insightful and caring can become self-preservationists. They must be careful whose feet they step on and keep the enemy list low and deliberate. They may intuitively want to care for the employees in their charge, but office politics and political survival becomes their main job. Some A Leaders feel so out of sorts with this behavior that they leave the company at the first chance they get (and good leaders generally get this chance more often). And those who dare to speak up about it suddenly find themselves leaving the company to "spend more time with their family" or "pursue other opportunities."

Culture strikes again. The ones who play along stay; the ones trying to change the organization are asked to leave, or are treated so poorly they leave on their own.

Brian P. Hogan, an author and software engineer, summed it up nicely in this tweet from 2018:

> I've had some toxic jobs. Lesson learned:
> When things go bad, good people leave, eventually followed by people who thought they could change things but got buried because too many good people left. Those left are bad people or hostages.
> The good people are your canary.

Leadership guru Peter Drucker calls an organization's resistance to change the "Cuckoo Effect":

> Any foreign innovation in a corporation will stimulate the corporate immune system to create antibodies that destroy it.

The Cuckoo Effect is the most difficult part of changing a culture and improving leadership.

Toxic Leadership Archetypes

In this section, we're going to go through some of the most common archetypes of poor leadership styles. These are labels I created to refer to collections of toxic leadership behaviors I often spot together. Some toxic leaders have traits from multiple archetypes. I suspect some readers will see this list and feel that I wasn't extreme enough. I feel for you.

Each instance of these types of leaders is likely to be a drop of poison in your company. The more you have, the more likely you'll also have a toxic culture, which we'll talk about in the next chapter. Before we start, I want to mention something important: The existence of these archetypes doesn't speak to the *intention* of those who practice them. Some of the styles you're going to read about could easily be adopted by well-intentioned people—maybe even yourself. Most leaders believe they're doing the right thing for their company and employees. They don't realize the long-term damage they're doing. See if you can spot any of these styles of management in yourself or your organization. In Part 3, we'll revisit these archetypes with tips on where to focus your attention if you do spot yourself in any of them.

The Chess Master

Core Beliefs:
- Leaders know best. It's their job to make decisions; it's their employees' jobs to respect those decisions.
- Employees cannot solve problems without guidance.

- Leadership itself is the reward.

The Chess Master believes that leadership is a position of control. Those who have achieved it believe they have earned the right to have and hold special information and knowledge, which is withheld from employees until it's time for them to know. This belief that leadership is privileged and hierarchical can sometimes be culturally influenced. Countries such as India, Nepal, Pakistan, Sri Lanka, Nigeria, and Japan have caste systems of varying degrees in their cultures, so leaders from these countries sometimes lead this way—which is toxic in western cultures. It's challenging to unlearn when it's demonstrated to you throughout your entire life.

The Chess Master treats employees like chess pieces on a board. They believe that their employees have nothing of value to add to big team decisions about topics such as processes, goals, team formation, team membership, etc. They meet secretly with a trusted inner circle to decide the fates of their employees in these areas, and only after they have made up their minds do they announce the changes to the affected team(s). Chess Master leaders are usually quite surprised at the pushback and lackluster commitment they get from their employees over these new plans. They're caught off guard when their teams don't think of them as the legends they believe themselves to be. The morale and engagement on a Chess Master's team are often quite low.

The Peacock

Core Beliefs:

- The way up is through demonstration of what leaders above me want to see.
- My employees exist to make me look good.
- Employees who excel at making me look good are loyal.
- Employees who don't help me look good are disloyal.
- Everyone who works for me should be loyal to me before anything else—even the company.

A corollary to the Chess Master type, the Peacock is an expert at making certain *their managers* see them as the most amazing leader since Franklin Delano Roosevelt. Meanwhile, their employees are mere peons whose sole job is to make them look good. The existence of this management style is just as much the fault of the Peacock's *manager* because this style simply wouldn't work if upper management didn't allow it to.

Peacocks have never heard a good idea that wasn't worth claiming credit for. Conversely, they're also very adept at shirking all accountability for anything that goes wrong. When sharing their teams' accomplishments upward, they're very good at stripping all the real value from the work until what remains is a carcass of three bullet points (always numbers) that win them the most points with their boss in the shortest amount of time.

These leaders often make the claim that they're "data driven," mainly because they use data selectively to show how great they are. That is, until the data shows they're wrong or that things aren't going well, in which case their ability to sweep that data under the rug is surpassed by no janitorial staff in existence. Their obsession with meaningless data with which to impress their bosses creates a situation in which the organization spins its wheels while substantive issues go unaddressed.

Peacocks often claim that their top value is loyalty. Rather than viewing loyalty as something they need to *give* to *receive*, they view it as something that is *owed to them*. Trying to escape these leaders is treacherous; they will view your departure as disloyalty, and depending on their height in the organization, they can sabotage your career from afar. If these leaders had a tattoo, it would read, "You either agree with me or you're against me."

Since Peacocks spend a disproportionate amount of time managing upward, they have little or no time left to manage downward. However, they are very good at critiquing what's happening below without taking any accountability for it. As an example of this, Barbara, whom I mentioned in the introduction, is a Peacock. When faced with terrible engagement scores (some of the lowest in the company), she called her leadership team into a room and asked them, "What are you going to do about this?" She was completely oblivious to the fact that *her* decisions and actions were what were so unpopular. Her direct reports tried to communicate that fact, but Barbara seemed to have a natural ability to let her own culpability go in one ear and out the next without a stop anywhere in her prefrontal cortex.

Peacocks' upward focus makes them adept at politics, and they will outsmart most efforts to dethrone them. This is especially true if *their* leaders are also Peacocks. If your organization is filled with Peacocks, it's time to run for the hills. I'm kidding . . . sort of.

Employees who thrive under Peacocks are—you guessed it—other Peacocks. Those who toe the line and make the Peacock leader look good are rewarded with promotions and special assignments. As these boss's pets get promoted, employees who actually care about the company begin leaving in droves.

The last thing to note about Peacocks is that they usually play the sideways game quite well. They are careful to maintain good relations with their peers, who have a seat at the same table with their common boss. It wouldn't be politically smart to have enemies at that table. It's not uncommon to hear from elsewhere in the organization that the Peacock is a great leader or good person while members of their own teams dread every waking moment at work.

The Ladder Climber

Core Beliefs:

- The work I do is beneath me. I deserve to be promoted.
- Projects that have high visibility are attractive.
- Projects with low visibility aren't worth my time.
- Getting promoted should be a checklist I can follow.

The Ladder Climber is a sibling of the Peacock, but there is a distinction in that they are often much more transparent about their motives. They make no secret of the fact that their goal is to get promoted. This results in awkwardness as coworkers feel like the rungs of this person's ladder are made up of their skulls. A Ladder Climber has difficulty creating trust as most employees feel like literal tools being used by this person to ascend a mountain.

The obsession with promotion is frustrating for everyone above, to the side, and below the Ladder Climber. Those above are constantly asked for the checklist of behaviors and accomplishments needed for promotion. Those to the side feel as if they're in a competition they had no desire to be in and are in constant fear of being thrown under the feet of the Ladder Climber so they can get just a slight bit higher. Those below are usually neglected because, just like the Peacock, the Ladder Climber's focus is always upward. If and when they are promoted, those they lead will rarely follow them; their disengagement will often be explained by the Ladder Climber with the phrase "people just don't want to work anymore."

The Micromanager

Core Beliefs:

- No one does the work like I can.
- The solutions my employees come up with are substandard.
- If I wasn't here, this place would fall apart.

The Micromanager is usually a perfectionist with trust issues. This is a leader who believes that they are the expert and their employees are the students. They pick apart their employees' work and very quickly decide it can't be trusted to be as perfect as their own. Soon, the micromanager goes full helicopter parent with their team—checking every detail, treating each employee as if they are a set of hands without a brain and, at the same time, complaining about how their employees never think on their own.

These types of leaders create their own self-fulfilling prophecy. When their employees are treated as if they are hands without a brain, those employees begin shutting down their brains—because, why bother? They're just going to get second-guessed, made to feel inadequate, and told they are wrong and that their ideas won't work.

Talented people leave these managers in a hurry and morale is usually quite low for those who stay. Innovation and engagement are usually low since most team members have stopped thinking or caring.

Sometimes Peacocks and Ladder Climbers adopt Micromanager behaviors. Getting involved in every little detail their teams are working on gives them the opportunity to claim credit for everything. When leaders act this way, it reinforces their belief that the team can't live without them when in fact most of the team desperately wants to give that a try.

The Invertebrate

Core Beliefs:

- Problems usually work themselves out if given enough time.
- I'm too busy to deal with conflict and disagreement.
- Good leadership means being friends with everyone on the team.

Managers with this style try to make everyone happy but end up pissing everyone off in the process. Their milquetoast approach to management leaves their bosses *and* their employees yearning for more spine. Invertebrates don't do conflict—so any bullying on the team will go unchallenged and the rest of the team will be left to fend for themselves. When they aren't burying their heads in the sand in the face of danger, they're usually making excuses for aggressors. They are everyone's friend and no one's leader.

Invertebrates attempt to assuage any unwelcome decisions from above rather than going to bat for employees. Their employees quickly learn not to bring issues to them because they know nothing will be done. Many get used to taking matters into their own hands when they need things. Invertebrates assume this means their team is highly functional when it's usually quite the opposite. As Perry Belcher, founder of DigitalMarketer.com, said in 2020, "Nothing will kill a great employee faster than watching you tolerate a bad one."

The Drill Sergeant

Core Beliefs:

- Employees are here to follow orders, not question them.
- If I wasn't here, nothing would get done.
- Employees want to collect a paycheck without doing anything. It's my job to make sure that doesn't happen.
- If you follow the process, it always works.

The Drill Sergeant is on the opposite side of the spectrum of the Invertebrate. Drill Sergeants are no one's friend and believe they are great leaders. Like Micromanagers and the Chess Masters, Drill Sergeants believe that employees are "less than" in some capacity . . . that people are inherently stupid, lazy, and only do what they're instructed to do when they're instructed to do it. They usually have short tempers, are quick to assign blame, and their motto is "yell first, ask questions later." Drill Sergeants believe that anyone on the team can be correct as long as that person is them. They've never met a problem that couldn't be solved with a process. When faced with low morale, these managers usually begin witch hunts to find out who needs the attitude adjustment. Their motto is that old standard "the beatings will continue until morale improves." They probably didn't get enough hugs as kids.

The Data Freak

Core Belief:

- Data is king. If the data doesn't show it, it didn't happen.

Data Freaks don't even get out of bed unless the data tells them it's the right thing to do. These people have trust issues. Data is useful but Data Freaks take data collection to astronomically useless levels. If they could, they'd install identity sensors in bathrooms to measure the productivity loss.

Data Freaks will proudly and repeatedly announce to everyone who will listen that they are "Data Driven." This translates to "I don't trust anything you say unless you can back it up with data." Usually what is behind this obsession is an inherent insecurity or imposter syndrome. By only making decisions that can be squared against the numbers, they protect their reputations. If a decision they make is unpopular or goes wrong, they can shrug and point to the data. If decisions are late, it's not their fault because they were waiting for the data. You wouldn't want them to rush into a decision without the data, would you?

In leadership roles, the Data Freak creates havoc in organizations by forcing employees to create measurements for obvious issues. Like an ER doctor who ignores the blood gushing out of your arm to ask someone to measure your blood pressure, bad things happen in the pursuit of certainty—or the illusion of certainty anyway. Resentment and distrust build in these environments, and employees often resort to just inventing numbers to satisfy the gatekeeping of their Data Freak manager to get things done.

In their pursuit of the almighty number, Data Freaks often jump over dollars to pick up dimes—and ignore *that* data in the process. They will gladly send their entire organization into a data collection frenzy—spending hundreds of person-hours gathering and analyzing data that will, in the end, likely be unable to save the company anywhere near the money it spent to collect all the information in the first place. But look at the pretty bar graphs!

The Bottom Liner

Core Beliefs:

- Business is business.
- Everything is measurable and connected to the bottom line in some way, and that is all that matters.

The Bottom Liner can easily disregard any negative outcome for others if it will help the bottom line. This type differs from the

Data Freak because rather than a general obsession with data, Bottom Liners are obsessed with *one* piece of data: profit. That means relentless cutting of expenses and growing revenue regardless of the long-term impact on the organization.

There is good data[5] to show that Bottom Liners manage to get *less productivity* from employees—even employees who are also bottom line focused. Why would that be? Because Bottom Liners give off the vibe that employees don't matter. The most important thing is the bottom line. Employees never trust that their own best interests are represented (and they are correct). As a result, they hold back performance. Why break your back for a boss who cares about profits more than they care about you?

As we enter a post-COVID world, I'm noticing a dramatic uptick in this reaction across organizations. Workers are increasingly disenchanted in the short-term profit at all costs mentality of capitalism—a mentality that proliferated during the pandemic. I expect that companies will struggle here the most in the coming years. More on this later.

The Squirrel

Core Beliefs:

- Ain't nobody got time for that.
- Faster is better, always and in all ways.

The Squirrel is often quite brilliant and successful, but they are moving so fast that they cannot hear others who move slower than they do—i.e., most people. A common way that Squirrels are received by employees is that they appear to have zero patience—the speed Squirrels are moving at creates chaos and disengagement all over their organization.

One of the primary behaviors associated with Squirrels is what I like to call Seagull Leadership. They are moving so fast and are involved in so many things that teams are often working

---

[5] Visit https://www.sciencedaily.com/releases/2019/07/190725130811.htm for more information.

without them around. Then, suddenly, they swoop in, shit all over what the team has been doing, then fly off into the sunset. It only takes a few of these occurrences for employees to feel disempowered and start shutting down their brains. Team members will put the brakes on new ideas or directions by saying things like, "We need to check with Alex before we decide this." Why? Because Alex has a reputation for being a Seagull. Congratulations Alex! You've created an approval gate for your teams, who will now pause and stare at their navels until you swoop in to make a decision about something you will frustratedly believe they should have decided without you.

I've worked with Squirrel leaders who are genuinely some of the nicest people you'll ever meet. Truly, they have the hardest part of leadership down pat. They care about people and genuinely lead from that place. The problem with the Squirrel style is that most employees don't feel heard by them. They raise concerns or ideas and are usually cut off and dismissed by the Squirrel's mind that has already rushed to a conclusion before the second sentence is uttered. While I'm certain that no ill intent is present in many of these cases, the result is that employees feel straw-manned[6], gaslit[7], disconnected, and/or not heard, and the disengagement in the organization begins.

The Graveyard Whistler

Core Beliefs:

- If I don't acknowledge it, it doesn't exist. Corollary: If I acknowledge something, it gives it power.
- Leaders must always appear strong and confident. Vulnerability is weakness.

---

[6] Strawman is a logical fallacy where someone incorrectly summarizes your position and then argues with that made-up position rather than your actual position.

[7] If you aren't familiar with the term, the word gaslighting came to popularity after the 1944 film called "Gas Light" in which a husband attempts to convince his wife and others that she's insane by manipulating reality and insisting that she's mistaken when she points it out.

A close associate of the Squirrel is the Graveyard Whistler. The term comes from the phrase "whistling past the graveyard," which describes a person unable or unwilling to acknowledge their own fear. They nervously whistle to pretend there is nothing to be afraid of. Graveyard Whistlers are toxically positive and ignore/avoid negativity whenever possible—seeming to live in what appears to others as a fictional world.

The difference between a Squirrel and a Graveyard Whistler is that a Squirrel doesn't have the time and/or attention span to learn about anything negative going on. A Graveyard Whistler is aware but avoidant of that negativity. Both types leave in their wakes burned out and frustrated employees who don't feel heard.

Graveyard Whistlers, like so many other toxic leader archetypes, are often well-intentioned. In their case, their core leadership belief usually centers on the idea that a leader shows strength through positivity and motivation rather than acknowledging difficulty. The problem is that connection is built through shared experience. When employees are concerned about the difficulty of a problem they're facing, Graveyard Whistlers tend to ignore or downplay that difficulty. This drives disconnection and damages credibility.

If this sounds like you, consider the deeper dives below.

DEEPER DIVE

The Power of Vulnerability by Brené Brown
Dare to Lead by Brené Brown
Multipliers by Liz Wiseman

When Things Get Clinical

The current estimate is that between 8–12 percent of executives[8] would likely fit the description of a sociopath or psychopath. The difference between the two is a matter of degree of conscience. Both act without an ability to feel empathy. When a sociopath swindles you out of money, they might feel a bit of guilt about it. A psychopath can do so without ever feeling any remorse.[9] Technically, these are classified as "antisocial personality disorders" (ASPD), and I suspect the percentage is higher if you include all the personality disorders that psychologists call the "Cluster B" disorders (Antisocial, Borderline, Histrionic, Narcissistic). ASPD is characterized by:

> [A] pervasive and persistent disregard for morals, social norms, and the rights and feelings of others. Individuals with this personality disorder will typically have no compunction in exploiting others in harmful ways for their own gain or pleasure and frequently manipulate and deceive other people. While some do this through a façade of superficial charm, others do so through intimidation and violence. They may display arrogance, think lowly and negatively of others, lack remorse for their harmful actions, and have a callous attitude to those they have harmed.[10]

Technically, there are three sets of psychological behaviors known as the Dark Triad that come into play with leaders. They are narcissism, Machiavellianism, and psychopathy. Narcissism is a centering on oneself over others. Machiavellianism is a belief that the ends justify the means. Psychopathy is an inability or difficulty in empathizing with

---

[8] Jack McCullough, "The Psychopathic CEO," *Forbes*, last modified December 9, 2019, accessed January 1, 2023, https://www.forbes.com/sites/jackmccullough/2019/12/09/the-psychopathic-ceo/.

[9] Kara Mayer Robinson, "Sociopath V. Psychopath: What's the Difference?" ed. Smitha Bhandari, WebMD, last modified February 14, 2022, accessed January 1, 2023, https://www.webmd.com/mental-health/features/sociopath-psychopath-difference.

[10] Wikipedia, "Antisocial Personality Disorder," Wikipedia, last modified February 5, 2021, accessed March 1, 2021, https://en.wikipedia.org/wiki/Antisocial_personality_disorder.

others. Often, some or all of these three behavior sets overlap in a single person to a varying degree. This is massively oversimplified and if the topic interests you, I strongly recommend the deep dives I've identified for this section.

It may sound a bit hyperbolic to say that your boss is a psychopath, but research indicates that those who exhibit behavior of the dark triad do tend to get ahead in corporations that value ruthless performance. These types of leaders often prove to be poor leaders in the end, however, because the very same lack of empathy and ruthless pursuit of power for themselves at all costs works against them once they reach the top or get near it. They don't use power for the good of others. The higher they get, the more that begins to show, and the more people it begins to impact.

It is no joke working for someone who has a clinical personality disorder. I worked five years for a company founder who had textbook narcissistic personality disorder (NPD). The experience ultimately sent me to therapy and to the doctor with a strange skin pain that was diagnosed as a stress injury—my nerves were literally being overstimulated from cortisol, the stress hormone. It disappeared just a few weeks after I was finally fired for standing up to him. Another employee at the company ended up with a pain injury that would not go away for months. When he left the company, it too vanished within weeks. This is serious business.

Being right is so important to those who have NPD, that I like to joke that they all have a master's degree in revisionist history. Inside the span of a single day, they can claim they said something they didn't, or didn't say something they did. In my dealings with my NPD boss, I began questioning my own memory, sanity, and self-worth. To avoid conflict, I had to be wrong even when I wasn't. I tolerated constant gaslighting.

NPD leaders vacillate between propping people up and then knocking them down. My former boss used to hire people he touted as brilliant (and "smarter than you guys," which is why he was supposedly bringing them in). Then, quite predictably, when they disagreed with him about anything, they were quickly let go, and the rest of us were told how stupid they were. He had childish, demeaning nicknames for all of us and for everyone we dealt with. I'm bald and he used to call me Charlie Brown. He thought it was funny. I thought it was like being led by someone stuck in middle school.

While this sounds extreme, it was also very real. These people can be quite charming in a Forrest Gump, "been there, done everything" kind of way. They can woo you with stories of grandeur and famous people they claim to know personally. My boss claimed to be personal friends with a famous CEO, and when that CEO died, he even faked a call from the guy's widow in front of us. Because their swagger and inflated belief in themselves can look like confidence and ability to the untrained eye, these traits can propel them to the top of some organizations, or they can end up as entrepreneurs in charge of their own companies (as in my NPD boss's case).

If you are suffering from NPD or the other Cluster B disorders, it's unlikely you'd identify it in yourself and you'd probably read this thinking it sounds nothing like you—which is why these disorders can be so difficult to treat. However, if you're working for someone whom you suspect has a clinical personality disorder, it's time to consider getting help and/or saving yourself.

DEEPER DIVE

Corruptible: Who Gets Power and How It Changes Us by Brian Klaas
The Sociopath Next Door by Martha Stout, PhD
Snakes in Suits by Paul Babiak and Robert Hare

Identifying Isn't Enough

Ok, we've had our fun. You had your "yep, that's my boss" or, if you're brave, a "that's me" moment. But now what? If you work for one of these types, or if you've spotted these behaviors in yourself, you're going to need more than a description of the behavior; you need a deep understanding of why these styles are so tempting, what makes them anti-patterns, what kind of damage they're doing to the company, and what we can do to root them out of our companies and ourselves.

The rest of the book is dedicated to getting those answers. In Part 3, we'll specifically revisit these archetypes through the lens of what can be done to break away from them, so if you spotted yourself, read on.

CHAPTER 2: TOXIC CULTURES

Company culture is not an HR function. It comes from the top.

– Dax DaSilva, Founder of Lightspeed

At every company I've worked at and consulted for, when I've pointed out an odd or destructive behavior, I've heard some form of the statement, "That's just the [insert company name] culture." I'd be willing to bet you've heard it at your company, and you may have even said it yourself. This phrase speaks to an apathy that everyone has about their ability to change the culture at their company.

I can hear your protests now. "Change the culture?!?" you exclaim. "Are you nuts, Sean? I can't change the culture here. It's way too deeply engrained."

I'd like to remind you that your company's empty buildings don't have a culture. Nor does the beautiful logo on the side of them. The culture shows up every day when the people do. That means that if we want a different culture at a company, we need to change the way the people show up—and potentially which people show up. It's both as simple and as difficult as that.

A Symphony of Bad Motives

When I was in my high school drama club, the actors and crew used to do an exercise before we went on stage. Eyes and mouths closed, we would stand in a circle with our arms crossed in front of us holding hands with the person on each side. In other words, my right hand would be holding the left hand of the person to my left and my left hand would be holding the right hand of the person to my right. The leader would start by gently squeezing the hand of the person on their right. The rule was, when you feel your hand get squeezed, you pass it on through your other hand.

It would usually start out very jerky and unpredictable. It seemed to take an eternity for the squeeze to make its way around the circle. But after just a minute or so, the group would inevitably settle into a rhythm. We could almost feel the anticipation of the squeeze and pass it on immediately. Soon the squeeze began to feel like a pulse—a heartbeat—of the team until we were all feeling and passing on the squeezing at nearly the same time every second.

It's difficult to describe the level of connectedness that emerged from that exercise. When the group dropped hands, actors were instructed to be in character from that moment forward. Crew went to take their positions, and just like that, we were a team with a mission to entertain an audience.

If you've ever had the good fortune of working on a healthy team, you've probably experienced a synergy and level of trust like this that is difficult to describe. If you had a family emergency and had to pass something to a teammate, you knew for certain that it would be done as competently as you would have done it, and they could count on the same from you if the tables were turned.

In a healthy work culture, your motives dovetail nicely with my own, and mine fit nicely with yours and others'. We have a shared identity which makes us *predictable* to each other. That predictability is a form of trust. It allows us to focus on the bigger targets our company's leaders have set for us—giving our competition a good whomping in the market, taking care of our customers in an astounding way, developing the next doodad that will transform society, etc. A healthy culture allows us to be focused externally on that shared goal. We're not worried about someone stabbing us in the back because we have teammates *watching* our backs, just as we're watching theirs.

In a toxic culture, these motives go the opposite way. Your motives seem self-centered, and because I know that you're focused on your own safety first, I know that *my* safety is something I need to worry about also. That brings my defenses online and my motives become self-centered as well. All around us, our coworkers are standing up their internal armies of defensiveness. Everyone is watching their own backs, which splits their time, energy, and attention between these survival instincts and trying to focus on the objective of the team/division/company. Trust is virtually nonexistent in toxic cultures. Without it, we must now survive the culture *and* deliver the larger company goals.

This is why toxic cultures drain the life out of us: *We're working two jobs at once!*

Easy to Build, Difficult to Destroy

I've seen cultures inside organizations shift from healthy to toxic in just thirty days because of a single leader. Imagine you're working in one of those healthy cultures where everyone is focused on the target and feels like part of a synergistic team. Pushing back on ideas from teammates and leadership is welcomed because it's seen as the best way to get the right solution, and no one is threatened by criticism or a better idea.

One day, your VP or your senior director decides to leave and is replaced by a leader who begins rewarding some team members and punishing others. The people being rewarded are the ones who agree with the new leader. The ones being punished are the ones pushing back. Pushing back is now treated as disloyalty—a career-limiting move. Ideas that don't originate from the leader are no longer welcome, and meetings that used to be full of rich conversation are now silent with this leader in the room (until *after* the meeting—that's when the real conversations happen). Within weeks, the culture has gone toxic. It's honestly one of the most tragic things to watch or be a part of career-wise.

Again, this is not always about intention. This poisonous leader isn't likely waking up every day and thinking, *Today I'm going to poison the team I'm responsible for!* People do what makes sense to them, and some people who have been given leadership responsibility have, unfortunately, no idea that what makes sense to them is toxic to a culture of teamwork.

I hate to tell you this, but if you're a leader sitting in a seemingly bottomless pit of disengagement, with toxicity all around you, *you* may be that poisonous leader. As the saying attributed to Raylan Givens goes, "If you run into an asshole in the morning, you ran into an asshole. If you run into assholes all day, you're the asshole."

Have no fear! Part 3 of the book is for you. There is hope if you're willing to do the work to really examine your motives and mindset for leadership.

Toxic Culture Ingredients

Every toxic culture is a soup with some fairly common ingredients. They don't all need to be present to create a toxic culture, but wherever a toxic culture exists, so too are many of these ingredients:

- Brilliant Assholes
- Internal Competition
- Silos
- Theory X Leadership Styles
- The Peter Principle
- Valuing Managers over Leaders
- Bottom-line Mentality

Let's explore each in turn.

Brilliant Assholes

In 2007, Dr. Robert Sutton, a professor of management science at Stanford University School of Engineering, wrote the book *The No Asshole Rule*. The premise is that bullying behavior in the workplace worsens morale and productivity. Sutton outlines two tests to recognize the asshole:[11]

1. After encountering the person, do people feel oppressed, humiliated, or otherwise worse about themselves?

2. Does the person target people who are less powerful than him/her?

Companies that are deeply focused on short-term performance over long-term health tend to employ and/or promote brilliant assholes—incidentally or intentionally. Brilliant assholes are superstars in their field, but they can tear teams apart from the inside. As we covered earlier, these leaders are sometimes operating without any empathy because they are

---

[11] Wikimedia, "The No Asshole Rule," Wikipedia.org, last modified October 17, 2020, accessed February 27, 2021, https://en.wikipedia.org/wiki/The_No_Asshole_Rule.

incapable of it. Wherever brilliant assholes are at your company, I can almost guarantee employee engagement will be low and teams will be highly dysfunctional and low performing.

The good news is that, through coaching, we can usually help brilliant assholes develop the skills to drop the asshole part and just be brilliant.

I once coached a dysfunctional team with a brilliant asshole on it. I interviewed team members one by one and it was clear that everyone thought this woman was brilliant, but she was also forcefully elbowing her way to being the leader of the team—a classic Ladder Climber archetype. Everyone above and below her was tired of hearing about how unfair it was that she wasn't in charge. She was constantly pressuring her own boss and boss's boss for a promotion. She was pushy in meetings and often shut down conversations by pulling "seniority." She resisted new technical directions because she wasn't as sure-footed in those. Overall, this resulted in a team that was very disengaged. They didn't *hate* her, but they didn't see her as a leader, and some privately confessed to me that they would leave the team if she were promoted to leader.

I sat down with her privately and asked, "You want to be the leader of this team, right?"

She nodded.

"Every leader has one thing in common. Do you know what that is?" I asked.

She guessed the usual things: charisma, courage, vision, etc. It's a trick question though.

"Followers," I said. "All leaders have followers, and you don't have any at the moment."

She was quiet for a moment and then she started to cry. For the first time, I saw a glimmer of awareness in her eyes, like someone had just turned on a bright light. I told her I was there to help her get what she wanted—if what she wanted was followers. But if she wanted a title, money, or prestige without the followers, I wouldn't be able to help her.

I worked with her to show her that she should view herself as more of a gardener than a chess player (more about this later). Her job wasn't to build great products, it was to create the fertile soil for her team to grow in so that *they* could build great products.

She was a fast learner, and she did eventually move up in her career (and no one left the team).

It doesn't always work out that way, unfortunately. A different team I worked with also had a brilliant asshole in the mix. Steve was known for blowing up in meetings, shouting at people, and blaming and shaming them.

After his outbursts, awkward silence filled the air. Sometimes the meetings would end prematurely after he stormed out of the room. He was the most senior developer on the team, but the more junior team members did not look up to him because of how unpredictable and unprofessional he was. The manager of the team was a classic Invertebrate archetype so he had trouble confronting the behavior—but that wasn't the whole story.

I did my normal interviews with team members. Before I got to Steve, I met with the manager and asked if I had his permission to be frank with Steve about the situation. He replied, "Please do. I'm at my wit's end and I'm close to involving HR at this point."

When Steve walked into my private meeting with him, I found him to be incredibly charming. He was calm, cool, and collected. He was reasonable and quite likeable. I had to double check the name on my notes. If I hadn't had testimony from team members to the behavior of Steve, I would have been sure I was talking to the wrong guy.

I told him that when I was younger, I had males in my life who were so good at repressing their anger, they were like teakettles. They'd simmer and simmer and then just blow up. I gave him an example involving my brother and told him that a therapist once described his behavior as "emotional terrorism."[12] You just didn't know when it was going to surface, so you were

---

[12] I should mention here that my brother has gotten much better about this over the years.

walking on eggshells the whole time. The therapist used an analogy with me that I explained to Steve this way: "Sometimes these people use an elephant gun to kill a squirrel when a .22 would have done the job."

Steve listened compassionately as I explained that his teammates were giving me universal feedback that he was exploding in meetings, and that the impact on them was described to me just like what I experienced growing up feeling fearful of my brother's temper. He was shocked. He asked, "Everyone thinks that about me?" I told him the feedback was consistent but that I was there to help him, not to punish him. He got quiet for a moment and looked to be deep in thought. Finally, he broke the silence. He told me a story about a former coworker he kept in touch with who had left the company a year before because he thought the company was so broken. When he got to the next company, he realized that the company he left wasn't broken—he was. It was quite an epiphany for Steve's friend. "Maybe that's me right now too," Steve said.

We left on a great note. I told him that I'd let his boss know that we were going to work on it together and that maybe as a next step, Steve could consider apologizing to the team and letting them know he was going to work on figuring out how to better deal with his frustration.

The next day, I came in and my boss called me into his office. "There's been a complaint against you and it's serious enough that I need to investigate it in case HR gets involved."

"Ok," I said, wondering what this could possibly be about.

"Apparently, Steve didn't show up for work today. When the manager called him, he was told that he wasn't coming in anymore and was likely going to resign because you told him he was a terrorist and talked about guns and stuff and told him his team hates him. It went up the chain and over to me. I know that doesn't sound anything like you, so that's why I'm getting your side of the story."

I gave him the context for Steve's claims and explained that I was attempting to get Steve to feel some empathy for those who were on the receiving end of his poor anger management.

Luckily, my boss believed me.

I quickly realized this was Steve's pattern. It's why he pulled out all the charm at the beginning of our meeting together. It's a classic example of a paradigm called "Victim, Rescuer, Persecutor." Steve saw me as a rescuer of the team and didn't like the fact that he was being portrayed as a persecutor (the one being rescued *from*), so he went into full victim mode. But victims need persecutors of their own, and whom could he use for that? Me. So, he completely twisted my words, repeated them out of context, and tried to get sympathy from the very people who were upset with him.

In the end, nothing came of the complaint against me. Steve had enough of a reputation of similarly portraying others unfavorably so that he could escape blame for his behavior. He did resign and, as I explained to the manager, I was completely confident that this would be the best thing to happen to his team—and even to Steve if he ever let go of the idea that he never did anything wrong. Without Steve in the picture, the team's performance doubled, despite the fear that their senior-most developer had left the team. Junior developers stepped up in ways they could not while they were standing in the shadow of the brilliant asshole on the team.

The cost of having a brilliant asshole on your team can be immense. It can cost you talent, productivity, innovation, effectiveness, morale, and more. In fact, it's so costly that, at one point, Netflix adopted an official HR policy called the "No Brilliant Asshole" rule (they've since changed it to No Brilliant Jerks), essentially saying that no matter how smart you are, if we discover you're an asshole, we have a nice severance package for you. They weren't kidding. If you charm your interview panel and get hired and they then discover that you are, in fact, an asshole, they will give you a decent severance package as early as your second month at the company. They know how expensive it is to keep a brilliant asshole on the team; the severance check is a bargain for the company in comparison.

DEEPER DIVE

The No Asshole Rule by Robert Sutton

Internal Competition

One of my least favorite management techniques, usually employed by Chess Master archetype leaders, is internal competition among and within teams. This technique, if widely employed, can result in toxic cultures very quickly. Here's how it goes: Leaders ask two or more teams (or individuals) to solve the same problem, often without informing either that they're competing. The misguided hope is that the best idea will win.

While I'm generally in favor of spirited, healthy competition inside companies *that already have safety*, this is about as unhealthy as it gets. I've been at a meeting where a team was demonstrating their solution to the other team who had been given the same mission and was there to demonstrate *their solution*, but neither team knew about the other. I could feel the tension, anger, and loss of trust in the room. No one likes to feel like a chess piece being moved around a board. Those who work for Chess Master bosses have this feeling *a lot*.

In another example, I once coached a team where the Chess Master boss gave individual off-the-backlog "research projects" to individual team members and specifically instructed them not to tell me, the coach. I only found out about it because the team consistently missed the goals they set as a team for their on-the-backlog work. One of the engineers finally fessed up in a meeting to being distracted by the side project work, causing the rest of them to say, "He asked you to do that *too*?!" Awkward! This kind of internal competition rewards peacock and ladder climber behavior, which turns the culture toxic very quickly.

Unless we're talking about a potato sack race at the company picnic, I generally advise companies' leaders to redirect their competitive urges towards, well, their competitors rather than employees. Doing so can be quite a rallying cry and have the intended effect of pulling teams together. There are some obvious exceptions like hack-a-thons and innovation competitions where internal competition is fun, but I'm sure you can readily see how those differ from the kind of competitiveness I'm describing here.

Silos

Competition, by its very nature, creates an "us" and a "them." This is a terrible dynamic inside a company's culture. When competition is institutionalized, silos are the result. Silos are the various groups inside your company who focus on themselves without regard for the company as a whole. Forcing teams to compete for the same dollars can exacerbate this.

Finance itself is often siloed at most companies. When there is no shared identity across teams, those teams optimize for their own benefit without considering the impact on the value being delivered *across all teams*. My examples in the previous section demonstrate intentional (but misguided) competition, but that isn't the only way competition shows up. Sometimes it's a natural outcome of teams having no safety. If they're going to get blamed for failure, they feel they'd better focus their efforts on themselves rather than servicing any larger goal. Competing for survival is still competing.

> ### DEEPER DIVE
> *Silos, Politics, and Turf Wars* by Patrick Lencioni

Theory X Leadership Styles

In the introduction (you didn't skip that, did you?) I mentioned that one of the research books I read was published six decades ago. In that book—*The Human Side of Enterprise*, published in 1960—Douglas McGregor put forth the concept he's best known for: Theory X and Theory Y leadership styles.

Both Theory X and Y pivot around leaders' assumptions about their employees. In Theory X, the leader assumes that the typical worker has little ambition, avoids responsibility, and is individual-goal oriented. They believe their employees are less capable and work solely for a sustainable income (externally motivated). Managers who believe this about their employees are more likely to use rewards and punishment as incentives. Like the Micromanager, Chess Master, or Drill Sargent archetypes, they tend to believe that the workforce operates more efficiently under a hands-on approach to management. Theory X inherently creates and depends upon an "us versus them" culture between leaders and employees.

Theory Y managers, on the other hand, assume employees are internally motivated, enjoy their jobs, and work to better themselves without a direct reward in return. These managers view their employees as one of the most valuable assets to the company. They believe that employees take full responsibility for their work and do not need close supervision to create a quality product. Theory Y managers relate to their employees on a more personal level, as opposed to a more command-and-control, hierarchical relationship.[13]

What we're observing in the past few years of increasing employee disengagement is that when leaders treat intrinsically motivated employees in a Theory X way for long enough, those employees become more extrinsically motivated. Quiet quitting, as it's been called, is really just a tit for tat situation. When we underpay employees, for example, we are saying to them, "Why should I pay you one penny more than I have to?"—so we shouldn't be surprised when employees respond, "Why should I work harder or for one minute longer than I have to?" When we remove all loyalty *to* them, we shouldn't be surprised when we

---

[13] Wikipedia, "Theory X and Theory Y," Wikipedia.com, last modified February 10, 2021, accessed February 27, 2021, https://en.wikipedia.org/wiki/Theory_X_and_Theory_Y.

get no loyalty *from* them. As I write this, most large corporations are in the process of layoffs despite record profits. This behavior will only increase disengagement.

If this is the first you've read about Theory X and Y, you may be having the same reaction I did when I first read about it years ago, which is "Are you kidding me? People knew how to treat employees as intelligent, self-motivated people *in 1960*? Why are we still treating them like cogs in wheels who need to be led around by their bonus checks?" So much for the idea that treating employees well to grow the company is some sort of hipster, trendy idea that millennials created.

> **DEEPER DIVE**
>
> *The Human Side of Enterprise* by Douglas McGregor

The Peter Principle

The Peter Principle states that people in a hierarchy tend to rise to their level of incompetence. They continue to be promoted because of their demonstrated skills until they reach a position where their skills are no longer promotion-worthy—leaving the world with a lot of people in high positions who are, at best, mediocre at their jobs. The phrase was coined by Dr. Laurence J. Peter and later explained in his popular book *The Peter Principle: Why Things Always Go Wrong*, coauthored by Raymond Hull. Originally intended as satire, it resonated with people's experience and made a serious point about hierarchical dysfunction.

Companies that have the Peter Principle in the mix as part of their toxic culture consistently promote strong performers into leadership positions without realizing that performing well in a job doesn't often translate into *leading others* to perform well. The worst part about the Peter Principle is how bad the outcome is for *everyone involved*. Even the promoted person is given the message that they are doing everything right. Why wouldn't they conclude that? They were just promoted for it! So, they double down on everything they were doing before, thinking they're playing the same game, without realizing someone just put them on the sideline as a coach. They're no longer a star player, they're responsible for making other players into star players, and the skills needed for this task are *very* different.

This toxic ingredient is in play at many companies worldwide and is one of the most common toxic culture ingredients I find. Maybe you know someone who embodies this principle. Maybe you *are* someone who does.

Valuing Managers over Leaders

> *Leadership is about taking responsibility for lives and not numbers. Managers look after our numbers and our results and leaders look after us.*
> —Simon Sinek

Let me be straight with you here. I strongly believe in results. Companies that don't make a profit won't be around for long. I'm not arguing that the outcomes of profits, good financials, strong stock performance, being efficient, beating competition, etc., aren't worthy of pursuit. It's hard to do good in the world through our companies if those companies don't survive.

If you can sense a "but" coming, you're quite perceptive. The problem is not the focus on those outcomes, it's the focus on them at the exclusion of the human beings who are achieving them and the sustainability of the planet we're all sharing.

We'll spend more time on this later, but company leaders who focus on the numbers above all create a culture where output performers are promoted (see the Peter Principle above). Most individual contributor jobs are not preparing you to lead people, they're just making you a better contributor. When the number of widgets you make is what's valued by your company, it doesn't take long for the company to be run by widget makers (managers), but not people who know how to lead and inspire widget makers (leaders).

This tweet from Simon Sinek encapsulates the mistake that leaders make about their responsibility: "Leaders are not responsible for the results. Leaders are responsible for the *people* who are responsible for the results."

Embracing this fully can be terrifying for many leaders. If I hold you responsible for the results, you're used to that, right? You didn't get to where you are by not driving towards good results. When I tell you that you're responsible for the *people* who are responsible for the results, suddenly you go into panic mode. The only tool in your toolbox for leading people is simply commanding them to do what's always worked for you. Since you will be held to account for the results, you take great control over how those results are achieved. It's natural human behavior. And it's toxic.

What if, instead, I held you accountable for the happiness of the employees in your charge who are responsible for the results? You can't command them to be happy. You suddenly need new tools—many of them—because people are complex. If learning and using these tools of care, motivation, and influence doesn't make you just tingle with joy, frankly, you shouldn't be a leader because *that is the job*.

Bottom-line Mentality

In 2019, Baylor University did a thorough study[14] of 866 participants. Half were supervisors and half were their respective employees. The study concluded that supervisors driven by a bottom-line mentality (BLM) fail to get top performance from employees (see The Bottom Liner archetype on page 14). The study found, among other things:

- High-BLM supervisors create low-quality relationships with their employees.

---

[14] Matthew J. Quade, Benjamin D. McLarty, and Julena M. Bonner, "Supervisors Driven by Bottom Line Fail to Get Top Performance from Employees," ScienceDaily, last modified July 25, 2019, accessed March 29, 2021, https://www.sciencedaily.com/releases/2019/07/190725130811.htm.

- In turn, employees perceive the low-quality relationship from their supervisors.
- Employees reciprocate by withholding performance.
- When supervisor BLM is high and employee BLM is low, the damaging effects are strengthened.
- When both supervisor and employee BLM are high, the negative performance is still evident.

That last bullet point is an interesting surprise in the data. BLM leaders fail to get top performance from employees *even when those employees also have a BLM*. Sit with that for a minute. Especially if you're a leader who focuses on the bottom line as a top priority and who thinks the ticket to success is to get your employees to also focus on the bottom line. (Insert game show buzzer here.)

The study's authors wrote:

> When supervisor and employee BLM is similarly high, our research demonstrates the negative effect on performance is only buffered, not mitigated—indicating *no degree of supervisor BLM seems to be particularly beneficial*. It seems even if employees maintain a BLM, they would prefer for their managers to focus on interpersonal aspects of the job that foster healthier social exchange relationships with their employees in addition to the bottom line.[15] (emphasis added)

In other words: When leaders treat bottom line as number one, employees realize they're, at best, number two. And they return the favor. Even when employees pride themselves on production, they hold back when their leader seems to care more about the numbers than them. It's not that bottom lines aren't important, they're just not as important as the people who make them possible.

The Toxic Soup Recipe

So, we've discussed toxic leadership and toxic cultures. Can you smell the brew cooking? Each brings out the worst in the other.

---

[15] *Quade, McLarty, and Bonner, "Supervisors Driven," ScienceDaily.*

Each poisons the other. To understand the interplay between culture and leaders, check out Figure 1.

	Healthy Culture	Toxic Culture
Healthy Leaders	Virtuous cycle. Leaders reinforce healthy culture. Healthy culture hires, promotes, and cultivates healthy leaders.	Healthy leaders are demoted, passed up for promotions, and leave or they learn toxic leadership patterns are the only way up and play along.
Toxic Leaders	Toxic leaders create fear and morale issues. They demote healthy leaders and promote other toxic leaders. Trust and safety fall. Culture can become toxic quite suddenly.	Where most companies end up if steps aren't taken to remove/retrain toxic leaders.

<u>**Figure 1**</u>

In my experience, and that of those I coach and interview, when you place a toxic leader into a healthy culture, it is more likely that the culture will be poisoned than the leader will become healthy. I believe that the reason this happens is that most companies are asleep at the wheel when it comes to their cultures, and most toxic leaders are oblivious to their toxic behaviors. The combination of the two leads to the outcomes I illustrate in Figure 1. Avoiding this fate requires that companies value hiring and promoting those with strong leadership skills over management skills. This needs to permeate the company culture and be vigilantly protected by:

- Judging and measuring the performance of leaders primarily by the satisfaction of their employees. This would include turnover, engagement, net promotor score,

and many others.
- Training and coaching for leaders at all levels, not just the most senior ones.
- A mechanism and the requisite safety for leaders to get help if they're feeling pressured to behave in a toxic way by the company's culture.
- A mechanism and the requisite safety for employees to confidentially report toxic leadership behaviors—even if those behaviors aren't breaking policy. This wouldn't be to get anyone in trouble, it would be to focus training and coaching resources where they're needed.
- Mandatory exit interviews of all departing employees at all levels, and regular meetings between HR and other leaders to analyze those interviews. I cannot stress this one enough. People don't leave their companies; they leave their managers. This is talent the company spent a lot of money to recruit and cultivate who is walking out the door. If they're doing so because of a toxic leader in their midst, exit interviews can be a powerful tool to spot them quickly. It's still too late but better late than never. Consider exit interviews a safety net should other indicators fail.

We've talked about toxic leaders and the cultures they create, and we discussed how toxic cultures churn out toxic leaders. These environments and behaviors are primarily driven by two illusions: the illusion of understanding and the illusion of control. In the next two chapters, we'll explore understanding and control and why it's so easy to fall into the trap of believing we can ever truly achieve them. We'll also discuss the freedom that comes from letting go of these illusions.

Chapter 3: The Illusion of Understanding

The greatest enemy of knowledge is not ignorance, it is the illusion of knowledge.

– Stephen Hawking

The first of the two illusions that leaders have about their environment is the illusion of understanding. If you're a leader, you may want to take a seat and grab a cocktail because this may come as quite a shock to you. Here it is, the ugly truth, introduced as the first of Sean's Laws:

> **Sean's Law of Altitude:** The higher you are in your organization, the less likely you are to understand what's really going on in it.

To be clear, we aren't talking about the financial performance of the company. Higher elevation leaders usually obsess over that and know it well. But financial performance is the trailing indicator of what's really happened in your company. If you're seeing that your company is failing to innovate, that failure occurred months ago. If that failure to innovate happened because all your talented people left the company and new talented people aren't applying to work for you, this all occurred one or two quarters ago.

The siren song leaders fall trap to when attempting to understand what's going on in their company is metrics. Our software systems are making the call of this song even more attractive. Metrics, metrics, metrics. "Show me the data!" the leaders scream from their Star Trek captains' chairs while staring at their digital dashboards. No need to walk around amongst the troops. They can see the whole battlefield from their office. I call this ivory tower leadership.

If you're a leader who thinks metrics can give you the information you need to be "in the know" about what's happening with your company, let me introduce a few reasons to doubt them, the most important of which is called Goodhart's Law.

Goodhart's Law

> *When a measure becomes a target, it ceases to be a good measure.*
>
> – Goodhart's Law

Goodhart's Law says that as soon as you put a target onto a measure that humans can influence, the measure loses its value. Human beings will aim towards those targets, but not in the way you can easily predict or control. Perhaps an example will help.

At many companies, the latest trend is an unhealthy obsession with a measure called "cycle time." Cycle time measures the time it takes to finish work from the time it's started to the time it's marked "done." The measurement comes from Lean, which has its roots firmly planted in manufacturing.[16] If we want to see the immediate impact of Goodhart's Law upon cycle time, all we need to do is set a target on it.

A company I worked with did just that. As part of his Objectives and Key Results (OKR) process, the CTO set a quarterly target for the organization of a 5 percent reduction in cycle time. Sounds reasonable, right? The best of intentions, I'm sure. What he was trying to communicate to the organization was "look for areas where you can improve your efficiency." Again, sounds simple enough but, at this company, high performers (read: those who meet their OKRs) were rewarded with higher ranking and bigger raises during performance reviews, so the CTO was essentially laying down a gauntlet. The engineering directors immediately set about telling the engineering managers that *their* quarterly performance goals (again, tied to their raises, promotions, ranking, and bonuses) now included meeting a 5 percent reduction of cycle time for their teams. Those managers began placing those goals on the team leads, who then began cracking the whip on the teams to start focusing on reducing cycle time. This led to conversations like this one during peer review (where one developer reviews another's code):

---

[16] I'll spare you the rant in this book but just know that some of these trendy manufacturing measurements make complete sense in production line work and no sense at all in knowledge work.

Sarah: "John, your code is working, but the way you've implemented it, it'll be much harder to add the feature we have coming up next sprint. There's still time in this sprint, will you change the implementation?"

John: "I hear you, but I can't do that now because if I do, it will make our cycle time go up."

This team created technical debt—more work that would need to be done later—to avoid increasing cycle time. Meanwhile, other teams at the company started taking shortcuts in their testing (quality) to get cycle time down. Most teams began just breaking the work up into smaller, dependent chunks that produced no value until they were all completed.

Presto! Shorter cycle times. The CTO was happy. As requested, his teams had reduced cycle time by 5 percent—at the expense of additional work, decreased quality, and slower value delivery.

As I'm writing this, a spectacular story is being reported in *Business Insider*[17] that beautifully illustrates Goodhart's Law. It seems some Amazon managers are allegedly hiring people they intend to fire later so they can meet "turnover targets." According to the article, Amazon leaders are given targets to turn over a certain percentage of their lowest performers.[18] But some leaders don't have any low performers they want to throw into the sacrificial fire pit, and they don't want to get rid of high performers, so they've begun *hiring new people just so they can fire them later!* In over a decade of doing this work, I've never seen a better example of Goodhart's Law.

Allow me to give you one more example. I've bought several GM vehicles new from dealers, and nearly every time I've been pressured to rate the dealership with five stars when I

---

[17] Matt Turner and Jordan Parker Erb, "Some Amazon Managers Say They Hire People They Intend to Fire Later Just to Meet Their Turnover Goal," BusinessInsider.com, last modified May 16, 2021, accessed March 15, 2022, https://www.businessinsider.com/top-stories-amazon-hire-to-fire-james-charles-lawsuit-wells-fargo-exodus-2021-5.

[18] This dreadful practice, with limited utility, is attributed to former General Electric CEO Jack Welch.

receive the inevitable seven-page satisfaction survey from GM—a survey which seems to have an unhealthy obsession about my dealer experience while demonstrating a seemingly passing interest in my opinion of *the car itself*.[19] I'm not sure what GM does to their dealers who don't score well, but the amount of pressure I've gotten from some dealers to give them a high score has bordered on harassment. The salesperson, the sales manager, and the finance person all stress the importance of it over and over. They spend way more time convincing me to *mark down* that I'm happy on that survey than making sure I am, in fact, happy. I suspect this, again, is Goodhart's Law rearing its head.

I once asked a senior executive in GM's customer service division how the survey got so long and misguided, and he told me he didn't know. He said the survey is a product of many departments who contribute questions to it. I suspect that because each department cares only about their own targets, the focus is on those targets while completely missing what GM really needs to know: *Are we making cars people like?*

Contrast that with my experience buying a Honda. They sent a much shorter survey which had a single question about the dealer. The entire rest of the survey was about whether I liked the *car itself*. Were there enough cupholders? Were they positioned correctly? What about storage? Headroom? Legroom? How did I like the stereo?

I don't want to understate the importance of Goodhart's Law in explaining why so many companies are completely dysfunctional. Most are just cesspools of conflicting incentives driving the wrong behavior in pursuit of the wrong objectives. Leaders trying to drive behavior through targets on measurements are playing whack-a-mole. Employees will trade important things to meet your targets—even jeopardizing other initiatives at the company they may not be aware of. Goodhart's Law means you will get what you ask for—even if it's bad for the company.

---

[19] This may happen at other brands too, but GM is where I've experienced it repeatedly.

Despite what you may believe, you cannot manage a company by target setting on metrics. The more this false belief permeates your organization, the worse it will be for everyone. Finance's targets influence HR's targets. HR's targets drive policies that unintentionally hurt retention and talent acquisition. Performance targets hurt innovation and quality . . . I could go on and on. The more human beings involved, the more complex and futile it becomes to predict responses to these policies and targets.

It's not that targets are inherently bad, it's that targets that are handed down from above are usually more susceptible to Goodhart's Law gaming. People tend not to game targets they've set for themselves as they don't see the point in it. Smart leaders set the direction they want indicators to move or carefully choose metrics that cannot be gamed that encapsulate the work. They let teams set their own targets on the ways they contribute to that larger metric.

For example, a senior leader may communicate that they want to see customer satisfaction scores increase. Each team then decides how they impact customer satisfaction and sets their own targets on their piece of that metric. Customer satisfaction is broad by design. It's impacted by product quality, customer service, and a hundred other ways that senior executive can't possibly keep track of and no one team can game. Allowing teams to figure out their own contribution to the larger metric and to set their own targets on those in service of that larger metric is healthy. It will result in improvements that would have been difficult to spot otherwise.

Measuring What Matters

Let's assume you avoid the trap of Goodhart's Law. You're still not in the clear because you must avoid the additional metrics trap of thinking it is possible to measure what matters. As the famous quote from William Bruce Cameron goes, "Not everything that can be counted counts, and not everything that counts can be counted." The illusion is thinking we can know what will count ahead of time or counts right now. Human beings are complex and unless you're running a company full of robots who sell to robots, there are quite a few human beings involved in the process of doing business. What matters to your employees and customers is going to elusively change by the day, the person, or an almost infinite number of other factors. You'll measure the obvious ones, but . . .

> **Sean's Law of Metric Hindsight:** There will always be metrics that you didn't think to collect, and they will have made all the difference in hindsight.

That doesn't mean you shouldn't make at least an effort to measure what matters. As I mentioned in the GM example, their seven-page survey focuses most of its questions on my dealer experience. From a GM perspective this makes no sense. If I love the car but hate my dealer experience, I'll just buy my next GM car at a different dealer. But even if I love the dealer, that won't help GM at all if I hate the car, because I won't buy another GM car from *any* dealer.

The moral is this: Make your best effort to figure out what matters. Avoid setting targets on gameable distractions to what matters. Then, accept the reality that what will end up mattering in hindsight will often be the thing you didn't think of or couldn't measure.

Measuring Frequency

If you were connected to a heart monitor, your heartbeat would be measured in real-time. If there was a problem with any single heartbeat, you would know it immediately. If only measuring the mind were so easy.

Most metrics are just snapshots in time. Measuring the output of a system as complicated as the teams at your company is like poking your steak with a meat thermometer. It's giving you the temperature *now,* but it's always changing. And while you're standing there with the barbeque lid open, you're letting all the heat out (slowing the cooking). Poke too many holes in the steak and it changes the moisture levels. So, good cooks choose a balance between checking the temperature too often and not often enough.

Getting this wrong while barbequing screws up dinner. Getting it wrong on teams screws up their productivity. They spend more time getting numbers for you than working on products. If those numbers have implicit or explicit targets, it's a safe bet that the teams are both distracted *and* gaming the system.

Engagement Surveys

One specific metric that can be very useful is the employee engagement survey. The usefulness of these surveys rests on a couple of steep cliffs, however. The first is frequency. Many companies do them annually, which means that employees have 364 additional days each year to feel differently, and these companies would likely never know about it. Some companies have taken to giving shorter so-called "pulse" surveys more frequently. Some even do a simple smiley face rating daily. In my experience, the right frequency is probably quarterly for systemic (above team) issues. Space your surveys any farther apart and you risk having the ground shift beneath your feet. Compress them any closer together and you risk survey fatigue, not to mention it may be difficult to make meaningful changes to the system in that time frame. Team level surveys can happen more frequently but should require less time to complete.

The second way engagement surveys fail is when leaders don't communicate properly before and after the survey. Before the survey, we want leaders telling employees how important their opinions are and what leaders will be doing with the results. After the survey, the communication needs to center on specifics that came from the results.

The third way that engagement surveys rapidly lose value is when the leadership team does nothing (or the wrong thing) with the results of the surveys. The only thing worse than not doing an engagement survey is doing one and then doing nothing with the results. There is no faster way to make it clear that no one on high is taking it seriously, and that translates to employees feeling like they don't need to either. But don't fall into the trap of Chess Master thinking. You don't want to take the results, go into a cave with your other leaders and come up with a plan, announce it, then roll it out. You want focus groups. Involve employees in the solutions. The rest of the organization is more likely to accept and embrace solutions that were vetted by their peers, and you'll likely come closer to hitting the mark on solving the actual issue.

Etch this onto a rock somewhere:

> **Sean's Law of Engagement Surveys:** The value of employee engagement surveys is directly correlated to the quality and visibility of actions taken by leaders because of those surveys.

At one company I worked with, over 65 percent of employees said they wanted more ongoing information from leadership about what was happening at the company. Why were decisions being made? What pressures were impacting the company? So the Chess Master leaders came up with a plan. They would have standup meetings in building lobbies once a month where the leaders would come together and speak to employees. So far so good. The problem is that they turned these into cheerleading sessions where leaders would take turns talking about big wins for the company. At the end, they would reserve a few minutes for questions. It was very awkward for employees to ask the pressing questions they had for leaders when they had just wrapped up celebrating wins. Eventually attendance dropped at these events and engagement scores continued to indicate the same dissatisfaction with leader transparency, and the leaders were mystified. Had they simply focus-grouped the solution they came up with they would have discovered quickly what employees wanted rather than assuming they knew.

Metrics Fixation

> *If you don't collect any metrics, you're flying blind. If you collect and focus on too many, they may be obstructing your view.*
>
> – Scott Graffius, *Agile Scrum: Your Quick Start Guide*

I have worked with and for many leaders who got metrics wrong—especially metrics that aim to measure or control employees. Companies that obsess about metrics are delivering a clear but unspoken message to their employees: "We don't trust you. If you are so sure of yourself, find me numbers that back it up." And that's where the real waste of energy comes in because a target has just been placed on a metric, and Goodhart is starting to rub his hands together in anticipation.

Employees operating in this type of environment will spend inordinate amounts of time backing up their intuition with data, again usually data that they game now because their egos are on the line. During that time, the company's competitors continue to innovate, star employees become frustrated and leave, and the cost of changing course increases as more and more time is sunk into building the case.

To reiterate, I'm not saying metrics are bad. I'm saying *obsessing* about metrics is bad.

Sometimes I meet employees who tell me they love metrics, but that love nearly always stems from the belief that their career progression is pinned upon those metrics. If a company rewards the numbers, employees may appreciate the "check the box" aspect that metrics provide. "See boss? I made the numbers. Now promote me." But it is highly likely that there is complex and important work being done by other employees that's no less valuable but can't be—or just wasn't—measured. These employees are upstaged—and passed over for promotion—by those who are busy meeting your Goodhart's Law targets. Over time, this results in a drop in morale of your most creative and innovative employees. Eventually, through turnover and attrition[20], you become a company full of target seekers and box checkers rather than creative thinkers.

Metrics are just as likely to be your foe as your friend. They sing a tempting siren song but offer only an illusion of understanding. Companies that truly grasp the difference spend their time and energy on learning to pivot quickly rather than on the fool's errand of getting things perfectly measured before they act.

---

[20] Turnover and attrition... now *those* are some worthy metrics. We'll come back to them when we discuss what to do about all of this in parts 3 and 4. We're still wallowing in the "what *not* to do" part of the book right now.

Chapter 4: The Illusion of Control

Relax. Nothing is under control.

– Adi Da

I often played the bad guy in my high school plays. I guess I had the look for it, or maybe I just didn't look like the hero. One of the things I learned from my director was that, while he was a pro at human movement (he was a retired mime), he didn't spend a lot of time telling us how to move. What he did was instill in us a deep understanding of who our character was and ask us to consider how someone like that moved. Often that would result in creative solutions that even he hadn't considered. He could have easily said, "Now stand here. Raise your eyebrow. Look into her eyes now." His title was literally Director! But he spent most of his energy putting us into the minds of our characters and telling us what that character wanted and needed. We did the rest and it felt more natural for us, which translated to a more convincing performance. His objective was to bring those characters to life, not to control our every move like we were his personal puppets on a stage.

This taught me a lesson about autonomy and leadership at an early age. Too often I see leaders behave as if they can actually control outcomes by controlling complex people and situations. This is the second illusion of leadership: The illusion of control. First leaders fool themselves into thinking they understand complex human beings and the systems they operate in, then they fool themselves into thinking they can bend them all to their will. Not only does this drive toxic behavior, it also burns everyone out.

I've used the word *complex* multiple times and I've chosen that word with intention. To understand why, I'm going to introduce you to a framework for classifying such things. Using this framework, leaders can more easily recognize the very narrow situations when being, well, more directive towards people is appropriate.

The Cynefin Framework

Developed by David Snowden, the Cynefin framework (see Figure 2) is a wonderful way to make sense of things. It defines five possible ways to think about situations or work: Obvious, Complicated, Complex, Chaotic, or Disorder.

The framework is divided in half with predictable on the right side (complicated and obvious) and unpredictable on the left side (complex and chaotic).

In the ***Obvious*** quadrant, things are simple. The relation between cause and effect is obvious, repeatable, and indisputable. All that's needed to deal with items in this quadrant is to sense what's in front of us, categorize it into something that has a best practice, then apply that practice. Baking a cake would be an example here.

In the ***Complicated*** quadrant, the cause-and-effect relationship requires expertise. Experts may disagree on best practices, so we're often using good practices here instead. Complicated items require us to sense what we are dealing with, analyze it, then respond. Planning is an appropriate methodology to work with complicated situations. Putting a vehicle on Mars is an example of work that is complicated.

In the ***Complex*** quadrant, we've entered the unpredictable side of the model. Here, cause and effect only make sense in hindsight. We need to probe, sense the outcomes, then respond. The right answers *emerge* in this quadrant through experimentation, not planning. Hunting is an example of complexity. No matter how much planning we do, we cannot predict when we will find a deer. We can only head out in a direction, look for evidence of deer, and respond accordingly.

In the ***Chaos*** quadrant, there is no apparent connection between cause and effect. In these situations, there is no time to think. We must act first, then sense what's changing, then respond. A terrorist attack, an explosion, or a collapsed balcony are examples of chaos. These are the narrow situations where people may need to be told what to do.

Finally, there is ***Disorder***. This is where we are when we don't know which of the four quadrants we're in. For example, in the seconds to moments just after a loud bang, we're in disorder. If it turns out to be a car backfiring, we place it in obvious. But if it was an explosion or gunfire, it's chaos.

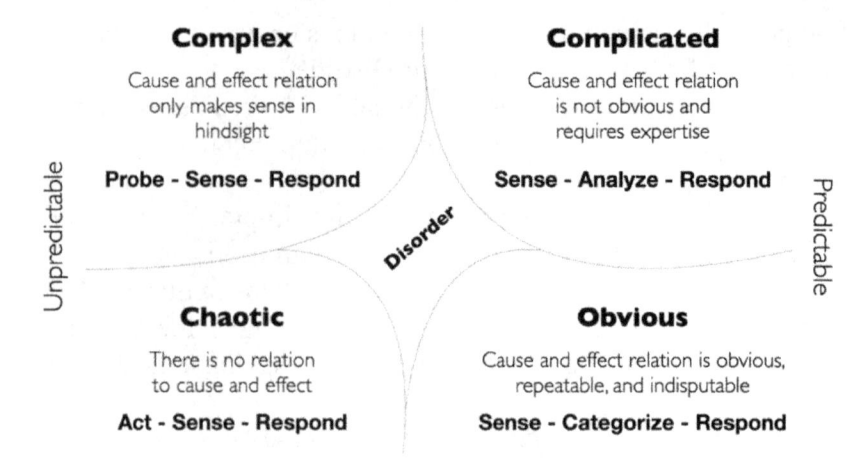

	Complex		**Complicated**	
	Cause and effect relation only makes sense in hindsight		Cause and effect relation is not obvious and requires expertise	
Unpredictable	Probe - Sense - Respond	*Disorder*	Sense - Analyze - Respond	Predictable
	Chaotic		**Obvious**	
	There is no relation to cause and effect		Cause and effect relation is obvious, repeatable, and indisputable	
	Act - Sense - Respond		Sense - Categorize - Respond	

Figure 2: Cynefin Framework

Now that you understand the framework, the word *complex* should make you think "unpredictable" and "experimentation," while the word *complicated* should make you think "predictable" and "planning."[21] A leader's actions are dictated by which quadrant they are dealing with. Just about anything involving human beings is complex. Since I'm assuming you're leading humans, you should probably buy a comfortable recliner for the complex quadrant because you're going to be there a lot.

The reason leaders have an illusion of control is because they often believe they are dealing with complicated situations, when in fact they are dealing with complex ones. Complicated situations *are* controllable with the right knowledge. Complex systems and situations, on the other hand, are always distorted by the evolution of the progress, confounding any efforts at planning. We can pretend this bull we're riding is a bicycle with streamers and a bell, but those two horns aren't handlebars no matter how much we want them to be.

---

[21] When someone is trying to get you to adopt an Agile mindset and processes, they are doing so because the work is complex and requires experimentation—something Agile teams excel at. Waterfall, on the other hand, is well-suited for complicated work like building a bridge because planning is possible.

The smart strategy in both riding bulls and dealing with complexity is to be limber and respond to change rather than following a plan. Great leaders know this, and they create environments where it is safe to experiment, fail, and try again rather than try to steer every employee through all the hazards using micromanagement and target setting.

Budgeting and the Illusion of Control

If you're in the finance department, you're probably not going to like this section too much. You see, your department is the first falling domino that makes the rest of the company both want control and think they have it.

Leaders throughout any company are all riding bulls—all dealing with complex employee situations, evolving markets, rapidly changing technology, competition moving at a fast pace, and much more. In the face of all that *complexity*, finance is there asking for these leaders to *predict* how many people they're going to need and which work they will be prioritizing, and HR wants to know who will be promoted for the next *twelve months!* It's lunacy.

The annual budget process at most companies is the one telling leaders that those bull's horns they're holding have streamers and a bell. While I'm going to discuss finance in Part 4, it's beyond the scope of this book to redesign the annual budget process. Luckily, I don't have to because the two fantastic books I've noted in this Deeper Dive do it for me.

DEEPER DIVE

Beyond Budgeting by Jeremy Hope and Robin Fraser
Implementing Beyond Budgeting by Bjarte Bogsnes

The Role of Trust

We can't go on without discussing the elephant in the room, which is the fact that many of today's leaders don't trust their employees. This is especially true when *their* leaders do not create safety to fail. If a leader's job performance is believed as dependent upon their direct reports' performance, it takes a strong leader to resist the urge to micromanage.

If you recall from our discussion of Theory X and Y in Chapter 2, trust is a crucial part of Theory Y leadership. Theory Y leaders know that the situations they and their employees face are complex and, rather than trying to pretend they can control them, they trust their employees to do the right thing and help them learn if they make a mistake. Theory X leaders view themselves as the ones with all the answers and their employees are no more than the hands they need to execute their solutions. That *might* work with complicated situations, but it's a recipe for failure with complex ones. In these situations, you need all brains on deck, not all hands. You need thinkers, not order followers. As Marty Cagan likes to say, you need missionaries, not mercenaries.

This chapter is a reminder for you as a leader that you're probably kidding yourself about the level of control you have over the systems, people, and situations in your business. But it's also calling on you to rise above the *desire* for that control. Do some stretching, sit down on that bull, and enjoy the ride.

Chapter 5: Toxic Communication

Communication is not about saying what we think. Communication is about ensuring others hear what we mean.

– Simon Sinek

I do listen. I just wait for the words to stop and your eyes to speak.

– Richelle E. Goodrich, *American Novelist*

Rounding out the toxicity part of this book, we will dive into communication. You may be a great orator or a great writer—many leaders are—but the kind of communication we're going to be discussing here is the unspoken kind, and many of us have huge blind spots in this area.

Actions Matter

We've all heard the phrase, "Actions speak louder than words." Some form of that phrase has likely been mentioned to you many times throughout your life—maybe something like:

- Talk is cheap.
- Put your money where your mouth is.
- Mean what you say and say what you mean.
- Talk the talk but walk the walk.

One nearly universal trait of toxic leaders is the perception that what they say isn't what they believe or what they will do. If you're not walking your talk, the impact on your employees is usually giant withdrawals of trust, gossip about you, disengagement, lack of safety, or perpetuation of the problem downstream (because *if my leaders don't care enough to follow through or tell the truth, why should I?).* This is what makes it *toxic* by the way.

The disconnection between your words and actions—not your intent—is what everyone remembers. This is an extremely important wakeup call. Well-intentioned leaders whose actions don't line up with their words tend to believe that their employees and customers see past their broken promises, empty visions, and hypocritical behavior because the *intention* was to follow through. This is simply not the case. A lack of follow-through always results in disengagement, regardless of your intentions.

Here are just a few examples of the kind of hypocritical communication many of us have experienced from business leaders:

- *"Your call is important to us."* Just not important enough to hire enough people to keep my hold time below twenty minutes or empower those people to solve my problem without transferring me three more times.
- *"Here in human resources, we care about you, and we care about our company values. If you see a violation, please report it!"* Do I really need to explain what typically happens after you report a violation? Spoiler alert: At most companies, if you're lucky, nothing. If you're unlucky, you'll wish you hadn't.
- *"We're reorganizing the company to streamline work and simplify the structure."* In other words, we're adding two new divisions, laying off a bunch of people who knew what they were doing, and replacing them with an offshore team in a new center we just opened in Poland. See? Simpler. You work out the details.
- *"As part of our simplification, we've reduced the number of VPs at the company by 30 percent."* We then hired or promoted another two dozen people into VP positions over the following six months.
- *"Employees are our most valuable assets."* Yet HR policies and finance budgets tie the hands of managers to respond to employee engagement issues by inhibiting promotions and preventing growth and lateral movement inside the company, and no one bothers to conduct exit interviews as employees leave.
- Jeff Bezos said in a letter to investors in 2020, *"[T]he large team of thousands of people who lead operations at Amazon have always cared deeply for our hourly employees."* Yet they have had 150 percent annual turnover among their hourly workforce.[22] Yes, you read that correctly. Executives are privately worried that the

---

[22] 1. Shira Ovide, "Amazon Is Brilliant. Why Not at H.R.?" *New York Times*, June 16, 2021, accessed July 14, 2021, https://www.nytimes.com/2021/06/16/technology/amazon-work-force.html.

company is running out of Americans to hire who haven't already rotated through the company's warehouses. Jeff Bezos is reported to have said that he doesn't believe in an entrenched workforce, calling it a "march to mediocrity," and encourages employees to leave by discontinuing automatic raises after three years and setting quotas for managers to let go of their bottom performers, a policy with long-term harmful repercussions, as we already discussed.

> **DEEPER DIVE**
>
> *Your Call Is Important to Us: The Truth About Bullshit*
> by Laura Penny
> *On Bullshit* by Harry G. Frankfurt

Perhaps if we interviewed the leaders who made the statements in the bullets above, we'd discover that they aren't hypocrites—that there is a perfectly reasonable explanation for the seeming disconnect between what they've said and done. I would argue that if such an explanation exists, one of a leader's most important duties is to share it with their employees and customers in a way that makes sense. Otherwise, you're just accelerating the drive down Disengagement Lane.

Remember those T-shirts that say, "Because I'm the mom, that's why"? Too many leaders today respond to the slightest bit of scrutiny using a "because I'm the boss, that's why" mentality. The reasoning sounds like this: "I don't need to explain myself. I get paid to make the decisions around here and this is the decision I made. It doesn't matter if employees think I'm a hypocrite or that it doesn't make sense. They can either get on board or go find another job."

If that's you, 1955 is on the phone and wants its leadership style back. Persist thinking this way and your twenty-first century talent is going to exit your company faster than Glassdoor can get the news (oh, and they will get the news).

Credibility: Your Most Important Tool

The United States dollar has value only because people believe they will be able to exchange it for goods and services later. Your word as a leader is only valuable if people believe your actions are going to back it up in the future. As a leader, everything you communicate to your employees is either effortlessly soaring on the trust you've earned through doing what you said you were going to do OR it's struggling to take flight because of past bullshit and broken promises. If you've got this kind of baggage, the audiences at your all-hands meetings will begin looking like a lot fewer than all the hands are in attendance, and those who do show up will be rolling their eyes and thinking "yeah sure."

Write this on a rock:

> **Sean's Law of Credibility:** Credibility is an effectiveness multiplier. The more you have, the more you will be able to do.

You will work twice as hard to lead if you're doing so with a lack of credibility. Your words will not shift anything. Your energy will be spent convincing instead of leading. Protect your credibility as if it is your most valuable tool—because it is.

There is no faster way for you to establish credibility than to painstakingly ensure that your actions line up with your words or thoroughly and repeatedly explain it when they don't. You can either do what you say, or you can stop saying things you don't mean. Either will help you earn credibility. People don't even need to agree with you; they just need to see you as predictable and trustworthy. If you believe your job as a leader is to lead people to great things, you'll need credibility among those you lead. If you think it's to maximize shareholder value and that people are just a messy necessity that you wish you didn't have to worry about, you are, unfortunately, part of the problem we're trying to solve.

PART TWO

THE COST OF BAD LEADERSHIP

The only thing worse than being blind is having sight but no vision.

– Helen Keller

Chapter 6: High Turnover

I literally just quit the project I was on this morning. I woke up to my boss's pettiness in my inbox. Welp, bye. I have a skill they're going to have a hard time replacing. I've got offers for other work if I need it. Companies need to realize, that leader they love so much is alienating good workers. There are other options in this world, and I am not spending my life groveling to a boss who doesn't even know what is going on. This 'scold first, ask questions later' management style isn't going to fly anymore.

—Comment on reddit

I just joined a new company, and within the first month I've had to evacuate due to Hurricane Ida hitting New Orleans where I live. I'm a remote worker, but my work has been super concerned with my safety and health (both physical and mental). They're providing me with resources, flexibility with my hours (since I had to drive to several different states to find a good place to stop and work), and concern for me that extends beyond 'can you do your job?' I'm new here, but that kind of actual and heartfelt concern for me outside of work hours makes me want to run through walls for them.

– Comment on the same reddit thread (followed by many commenters asking for the name of that company)

Companies are in business to make money. I hear this all the time as a defense for horrendous leadership behavior. Setting aside the idea that companies may want to consider additional reasons to be in business—an idea we'll return to later—I find it quite astounding that even these "maximize profit" types rarely consider the cost and profit ramifications of toxic leadership.

In this part of the book, we're going to look at some of the hidden and not-so-hidden expenses of getting leadership wrong. And we're not talking about pennies here. For large organizations we're talking about many millions of dollars. For small- to medium-sized startups, we could be talking about outright survival.

I recognize that some of my readers are all about the numbers and, if you're yearning for data about this topic, I've got you covered with the Deeper Dive below.

DEEPER DIVE

Our Least Important Asset: Why the Relentless Focus on Finance and Accounting Is Bad for Business and Employees
by Peter Cappelli

A Leadership Problem

I mentioned in the last chapter that Jeff Bezos is quoted by former executives at Amazon as believing that the road to mediocrity is paved by long-term employees. He likes and encourages turnover. Like a productivity addict who's never quite convinced that he has the most energetic and excited employees to squeeze for productivity, he seems to prefer freshness over depth, zealousness over institutional wisdom. Not in himself, of course; he led the company for *twenty-seven years* before handing the reins over to Andy Jassy in 2021.

The story of Bezos's relationship to freshness—and how it doesn't apply to him—is also the story of what's wrong with leadership today. Bezos was fine for twenty-seven years in his role because that role was challenging, exciting, and filled with direct financial rewards connected to his success. Most people who have those stimuli can remain quite engaged, motivated, and innovative at a single company for decades. If a company continually treats you as though you're a cog in a wheel and makes no attempt at feigning even the slightest bit of interest in your job satisfaction or career progression, in contrast, it can be a bit difficult to stay motivated or bring superior performance for long periods of time. To his credit, Bezos has solved immense logistical problems to move goods. But he apparently can't figure out how to treat employees well enough to get them to perform for any lengthy period, so he does the next best thing: he replaces them when they get stale.

Bezos and CEOs like him would like you to believe that high turnover represents a failure of work ethic from employees who are lazy or self-serving. In fact, it's their (self-serving) failure of leadership at a massive scale that's culpable.

There's an old joke about a worker who sees his CEO in an expensive sportscar and says, "Wow, I love your car!" and the boss replies, "If you work hard, put extra hours in, and strive for excellence, I'll get another one next year." As I write this, Richard Branson and Jeff Bezos have successfully gone to space and back. I'm sure if everyone puts in the hours, they and their wealthy buddies can buy another spaceship.

High turnover is highly influenceable—if not directly controllable—by company leadership in most cases. Leaving a job and starting a new one is, for most people, one of the most anxiety-inducing things they can do. It ranks fourth on the list of stressful events after death of a loved one, separation or divorce, and getting married. Many people would love working for the same company until they retire if that company treated them with even a tiny fraction of the challenge, growth, and money that Bezos gave himself as CEO, and now gives himself as chairman, of Amazon.

Turnover Is Expensive

I once interviewed a brilliant human resources director for a large healthcare organization. He told me that his most important piece of data was employee engagement. If he saw those numbers dropping, he'd go immediately to the leader in those organizations. These leaders were then coached and put on a watch list. His group wouldn't just take the leader's word for it when they claimed they were improving. They'd interview actual employees and ask them, "Your leader said they've improved in this particular area, are you feeling that?" When I asked him why he took the situation so seriously he replied, "Sean, I have hundreds of surgeons, doctors, and nurses working here. They represent a lot of invested money in recruitment, training, and relationship building. I can't afford to have a single jackass in a leadership position over these people causing them to leave. I'm not just protecting the employee here; my job is to protect the company from financial loss by way of losing valuable employees who are hard to replace."

I wish more company leaders saw this connection. Conservative estimates say that replacing an employee costs 150 to 200 percent of that employee's salary. That means every time someone leaves your company, you could have almost hired *an additional person* for a year for the money you will spend to replace them. Turnover is estimated to be over 20 percent for the tech sector. Let's make that real. If we assume that your company has one thousand employees and that the average salary is $150,000[23], that means your total salary cost is $150 million. If you have a 20 percent turnover rate and it costs 200 percent to replace those people, that works out to two hundred employees being replaced per year at a cost of $300,000 per employee for a total of $60 million. This is $30 million more than the salary of those 200 people had they stayed. You could have hired an additional *two hundred employees* at $150,000 each for the same cost as replacing the ones that left.

---

[23] Keeping things simple here. The actual cost of an employee is more than just their salary. In some ways, that makes the outcomes of this example even worse.

Still not convinced? What if I told you that the impact of turnover on your company wasn't "just" a few large expenses, but it also resulted in an increased workload for the remaining eight hundred employees in our example while you searched for and trained those two hundred replacements? Those who didn't leave either burn out or must put important work on hold because they can't keep up. That breaks dependencies across the organization, resulting in forced replanning and evasive action for multiple teams. If teams work longer hours to keep up, quality drops. But since the team structure has each team delivering only a portion of the product, the quality problems aren't discovered until the whole system comes together at the end.

All of this results in *more* turnover as people get tired of the pressure and doing the job of two for the pay of one. To add insult to injury, new hires are often brought in at higher pay rates and job titles than their teammates because, for some reason, hiring budgets are higher than raise/retention budgets. This further puts the morale of existing teams into a tailspin. But we're just getting started. Even after the new person is hired, people who can do the job must slow down to teach that person how to do the job that the person who left already knew how to do. Remember, in some cases, this new trainee is one of the highest paid people on the team now being trained by those who have been there longer. And this training can take weeks or months.

If the person who left was respected and admired, their departure leaves your remaining employees demoralized. The constant churn, meanwhile, keeps resetting your teams back to the forming stage of Tuckman's forming, storming, norming, and performing model, ensuring that none of them reaches performing. I've simply lost count of the number of leaders who ask me to get their teams to become "high performing" while they do nothing about turnover and constantly reorganize. They're asking for the performing stage despite doing everything in their power to keep the teams (re)forming.

Why Companies Ignore Turnover

In the face of all this, you may be asking how it could possibly be that so many companies would continue to minimize or downright ignore their turnover. I believe there are three reasons:

1. They believe employees leave regardless of what leaders do.
2. They're glad these employees left. The official HR term is "non-regrettable" or "positive" attrition.
3. They don't have a clue how to fix it because understanding human psychology is "hard."

Employees Will Leave No Matter What Leaders Do

This is the hands-up surrender to the problem. Setting a goal to reach 0 percent turnover is likely a fool's errand because it's true that there are some employees who will leave no matter what a company does. There are legitimate reasons for people to leave companies that have nothing to do with things the company can control, but this doesn't represent close to the 20 percent turnover rate we're seeing. As has been widely reported by prominent business journals for years, the data we have shows that people don't leave their companies, they leave their managers.

A Gallup poll of more than seven thousand US workers found that, of workers who left their jobs, over 50 percent did so to get away from a bad manager—but that's not the whole story. A different Gallup study found that of the reasons people stated for leaving a company, 79 percent were elements of the job that were *influenceable by leaders*. Here are the top five reasons people stated as the reason they left:[24]:

---

[24] Jennifer Robison, "Turning Around Employee Turnover," Gallop, last modified May 8, 2008, accessed December 10, 2021, https://news.gallup.com/businessjournal/106912/turning-around-your-turnover-problem.aspx.

1. Career advancement or promotional opportunities (32 percent)
2. Pay/benefits (22 percent)
3. Lack of fit to job (20 percent)
4. Management or general work environment (17 percent)
5. Flexibility/scheduling (8 percent)

More recent data has moved "Management or general work environment" up to number one. When I look at the above reasons, I don't see any that leadership can't influence, do you? All this data clearly debunks the idea that voluntary turnover is outside the control of companies and their leaders.

The Problem with Non-Regretted Attrition

If you were in a relationship with someone you loved and they left you because of your behavior, it would be very tempting to think, "Good riddance." Especially if, towards the end of the relationship, they were squawking a lot about your shortcomings. The problem with that attitude? While it might make you feel better, it won't set your next relationship up for success if there are things you could improve.

There is a natural progression of engagement at work, and it follows a similar pattern. It can be quite tragic for both the company and the employee. Imagine that you have a new hire. They are full of fire and excitement for the company's just cause, their new job, and their new coworkers. They're also holding back any judgment about anything negative they encounter. Usually this is because they're trying to give the company and its people a chance, but they're also trying not to rock the boat too hard since they're the new person.

Over time, these employees become increasingly aware that the negativity they're encountering is not coming from them, it's coming from the company. And because they're no longer new, they become more outspoken about wanting to change things. Read these next words carefully: *These are your most engaged employees*. Engagement doesn't mean happy; it means caring about mutual success. Like your lover who was calling you out on your behavior, these employees complain the loudest because they care the most about the company. But they're also the biggest pains in the ass for leaders who are, themselves, disengaged or who feel like changing things is too hard.

After some time of trying to improve things without success, these employees give up. Like a dying star, they flame out. It is *then* that they are disengaged. This is when they become outspokenly cynical and/or passive aggressively quiet. It's also usually right about when the organization demotes, poorly reviews, writes up, or otherwise punishes this employee. The employee leaves (or is asked to leave) as a result and the organization sighs and says, "good riddance." This becomes non-regretted turnover. Isn't that convenient?

Certainly, there are employees who get through every hiring process who aren't a good fit or who turn out to have real character flaws that are damaging to team synergy. Some have terrible work ethics or have misled the company about their skills. These may be correctly classified as non-regretted turnover, but I suspect that many who are labeled troublemakers are actually flamed-out employees who really cared a lot at one point. Because companies label these departures as non-regretted, however, they don't even conduct exit interviews or look inward to what might need to change, so nothing improves for new or existing employees and the dysfunction continues.

What if your company culture is repelling the most passionate workers in this way? What if the only people sticking around are the ones who won't make you a better company?

Human Psychology Is Hard

Whether they admit it or not, many leaders are completely out of their league when it comes to motivating human beings. As I mentioned, they may have been promoted into leadership because they were good at making widgets. Now their job is to motivate other widget makers, and those skills look nothing like making widgets. So, they throw up their hands and cover up their lack of leadership skills by blaming employee disloyalty for the high turnover—tossing money away in the process.

To describe the problem, I want to call attention to Abraham Maslow's Hierarchy of Needs (see Figure 3).

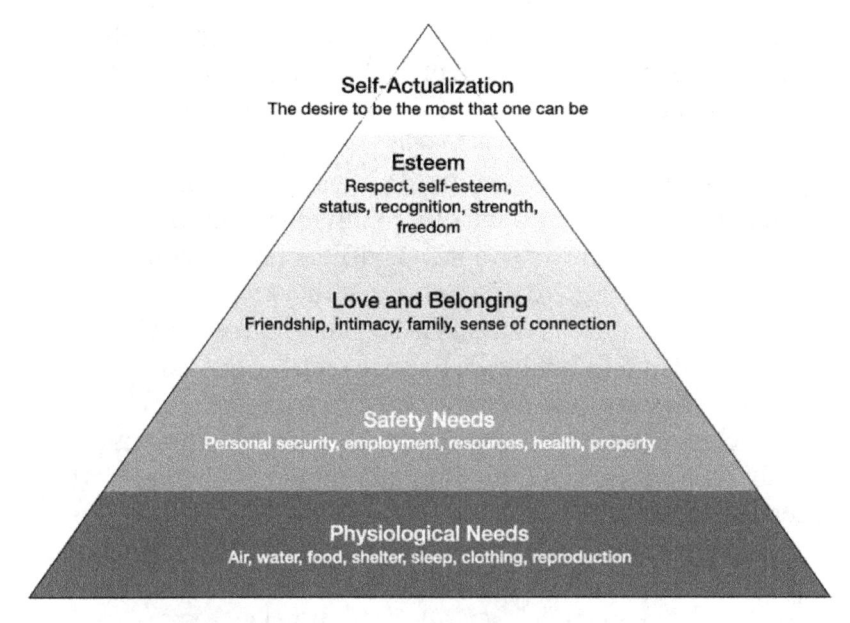

Figure 3. Maslow's Hierarchy of Needs

It's important to point out that there are critics of Maslow's hierarchy—especially the higher levels—but we're only going to be talking about the first few layers here where the science is relatively sound.

Maslow's hierarchy proposes that personal development follows a hierarchy. That, generally speaking, no one will care much about recognition (Esteem) when they're starving for oxygen or food (Physiological Needs). For the purposes of our discussion here, notice how low employment is on the pyramid. It's among the second most important human need: Safety. That is why changing jobs is so anxiety-producing for humans and why we can't ignore the impact we're having on employees psychologically by toying with their job security as so many companies do today.

Daniel Pink's work around human motivation holds Maslow's first two levels as prerequisites. According to Pink, people are incentivized by money only to the degree that it is "off the table." There's a bunch wrapped up in here, but it basically means they want to feel as if they're paid at or above their peers in their *field*, not just at their company, and that they are above the second level of Maslow's pyramid. What it takes to progress beyond the Safety level varies depending on geography, cost of living, and other individual factors such as family size. In short, when money is off the table, people aren't thinking about it, they're thinking about the work.

Pink's research shows that people who have their physiological and safety needs met are then motivated by autonomy, mastery, and purpose. Autonomy is the desire to be self-directed. Mastery is the desire to become an expert at something. Purpose is a desire to make an impact on the world in a meaningful way.

In Part 3, we'll discuss how leaders can provide what employees need to achieve these goals. For now, it's enough to know that *this is the work of leadership*. Whatever else you believe it to be, it is all second to the work of motivating employees. Without motivated employees, it is expensive—and often impossible—to accomplish anything beyond the most repetitive manual tasks.

DEEPER DIVE

Drive: The Surprising Truth About What Motivates Us
by Daniel Pink

Reputation Loss

I have never worked on a team that allowed so much animosity and hatred amongst coworkers and I do not say this lightly. Poor team management not only caused a toxic work environment for much of the staff, but also led to the department being inefficient and a money drain for the company. If leadership had stepped up

> *and actually problem-solved issues with the department, I would still have a job.*
>
> – Glassdoor review

If you're a leader who is noticing that good candidates are getting harder to find, you cannot ignore the impacts of negative reviews on sites like Glassdoor, Levels.fyi, Candor, Blind, and apps like Fishbowl. The reputation of your company is a living thing. When you have happy employees, their social circle gets regular doses of how happy they are and what a great place it is to work. Talented employees who take pride in their companies are not only happy to recommend their places of work to their talented friends but act as recruiters for those companies. After all, why wouldn't a talented person want to work with other talented people? Conversely, when an employee is frustrated with their job—sometimes long before they leave—their social circle gets regular doses of why they are dissatisfied. Anyone they know who was thinking of working for you will have second thoughts.

Most companies are aware of the statistic that unhappy customers will tell nine to fifteen others about their bad experience. What makes us believe that bad employment experiences are any different? I suspect too many companies are grossly underestimating the reach and impact their *current* employees have on *prospective* employees in a digitally connected world.

The more talented your employees are, the more connected they likely are to their industry. They have classmates from their alma mater (read: other star talent that you and your competitors are fighting over). They get together on weekends. They post updates to their nonlocal friends on social media. They are likely influencers in their field. They may attend conferences and socialize with others whose first questions are around their work. All this amounts to an exponential spread of your company's reputation—for the better or worse—one conversation/post at a time.

If these conversations lead to talented people not applying, they are part of the papercuts that kill companies in a slow-bleed fashion. Perhaps it's because each cut is so small that we fail to see the larger wound. It's also easy to miss the problem because we can't see what *didn't* happen. We don't know who thought about applying but didn't. The closest we get to knowing is when someone either turns down an offer, accepts and then changes their mind, or leaves soon after starting a position at your company for a different job. For every one of those, I estimate that companies with bad reputations have five they would have loved to hire who chose not to even apply.

We're going to discuss the cost of losing your innovation edge next but suffice it to say that it will be difficult for your company to innovate past your competition if the only people you can attract are the people your competitors won't hire.

CHAPTER 7: LOSS OF INNOVATION

You may be able to "buy" a person's back with a paycheck, position, power, or fear, but a human being's genius, passion, loyalty, and tenacious creativity are volunteered only. The world's greatest problems will be solved by passionate, unleashed "volunteers."

– David Marquet, Author of *Turn This Ship Around!*

When a company loses its competitive edge, there is rarely a warning. It's not like there is a line item on a financial report called "innovation" or "number of innovative employees" that an executive can see falling quarter over quarter and respond. The first sign that it has occurred is often the press release from one of your competitors announcing *their* new innovation or patent and you silently asking, *Why didn't our people think of that?*

Five Ways to Lose Your Innovation Edge

There are typically five ways that companies lose out on innovation from their employees:

1. **Ignoring the fire during hiring.** Leaders hire for pedigree rather than discovering and matching a candidate's "fire" with their job duties.

2. **Poor promotion and skill matching.** Employees have skills and interests that employers don't know (or care) about, so they aren't benefiting from them.

3. **Burnout.** Employees aren't giving you their shower time. Don't worry. I'll explain that one.

4. **Fear of Failure.** Innovation requires trial and error. When talented employees don't feel safe to fail, they don't try new things.

5. **Brain drain.** The most innovative and talented employees are leaving your company and taking their knowledge and ideas with them.

Ignoring the Fire During Hiring

There is a saying that smart leaders hire slow and fire fast. What this really means is that they are looking for skills *and* team fit, not skills alone. Since that combination takes time to find and assess, hiring is slower. If someone slips through that process and reveals themselves not to be a good fit, the leader recognizes that it serves no one to hold onto the person—at least in that role.

During the hiring process, some leaders become so obsessed with pedigree that they miss the opportunity to discover the fire burning behind the eyeballs of the candidate—the thing that really lights them up. Sometimes it's a type of work, a kind of challenge, a style of leadership (pro tip: it usually involves mastery, autonomy, and/or purpose).

Once you discover their fire, you may realize the candidate is better for a different position and give them a referral to one of your peers. Sometimes you realize that the fire is a perfect fit for a project you have but it's not the one you were thinking of when you opened the position. And sometimes you realize that their fire isn't a fit for your company. What's not ok is ignoring the fire. You can hire anyone to do anything but if you want their passion and innovation, you've got to respect the fire. If you have great interview questions about the fire but can't find one in the person, you may want to consider passing on them. Likewise, if you spot the fire but cannot offer this person a way to use it, do both of yourselves a favor and let them know this. You are preventing a future turnover.

I always like to begin interviews by saying:

> "Making sure we're a good match is really important to the company and to me personally. We want to make sure you're challenged and have an opportunity to grow in ways that also support innovation at the company. If we mess this up now, we'll both be unhappy, and you may want to leave. The only wrong answers here are you telling me what you think I want to hear instead of what's real for you. Does that make sense?"

Only after I feel that we're on the same page do I launch into my questions.

Potential questions:

- "If money wasn't an object and time was available, what skill(s) would you want to master and why?"
- "Is there a professional mark you want to make on the

world? If so, what is it?"
- "What work-related skills/talents do you have that you don't think we would care about?"

Questions like these invite the candidate to step outside of the résumé/CV pedigree conversation and into who they are as people. As the David Marquet quote I shared at the opening of this chapter says, you can hire someone's hands, but they have to *volunteer* their spirit and passion. Innovators love what they do, and people who love what they do innovate. So, don't just "fill the slot." Find the fire and connect it to their work for you—even if it means altering the job duties slightly. As I've said, leadership is more like gardening than playing chess. Your job is to create fertile soil for the plant in front of you, not force it into whatever plot of ground you have an opening for. It's the plant that does the growing and creating after that.

Poor Promotion and Skill Matching

Sometimes we discover the fire in our employees *after* they've been hired. They may tell us about a different team they want to work for, a challenge they want to pursue for the company, or discuss a restlessness they're feeling. As leaders, it is our job as representatives of the company to make sure we get the fire connected to the right place in the company. If we selfishly hold them back because we don't want to lose them on the team, we hurt everyone involved—including the team and the company. Ultimately this person will leave anyway but, in the meantime, they've checked out mentally. You've got their hands but not their passion.

If one of your star performers wants to move on to higher or different ground at the company, supporting them is the absolute best course for them and the company.

I will give one caveat here, however. I once worked for a company that was very stingy with handing out individual contributor promotions. Engineers saw management as their only path to getting more money—even though many of them didn't have a clue how to be good leaders—and many claimed to have a fire for a leadership role, but they really wanted the money. As a result, the company had a whole lot of poisonous leadership going on and many engineers left the company.

If the entire reason for your employee's upward yearning is more money, you're going to want to have a serious sit down with them (and perhaps revisit how they could get more money while staying where they are). Money alone is the wrong reason to pursue a leadership role. Don't perpetuate a bad leadership problem at your company by promoting people into leadership roles whose fire isn't about being good "gardeners" for other people's careers.

Sometimes employees want to move laterally at the company because another team does work that's more in line with their fire. If that's the case, support that movement. For example, let's say you have a talented developer working for you and find out that one of her hobbies is photography. She's thinking of applying to be a product photographer in the marketing department. This is a huge leap for her—a career change. But that's where her fire is. Why make her change careers *and* companies if you know she's a good employee?

Companies that "get it" have policies in place to move their employees to where their fire lies—even if neither of you knew about it at the time of hire. This includes policies that would allow the marketing department, in this example, to hire someone internally at a lower level and mentor them upward.

Burnout

Early in my career, I worked for a company that did event planning for other companies. They were basically giant party planners. My team of developers was responsible for creating and customizing the registration sites for these events.

One of the challenges the entire industry had was matchmaking for hotel stays. To save money, some companies asked employees to pair up in hotel rooms for conferences. The practice has fallen out of favor for a variety of reasons now but was quite popular during this time. Imagine the many variations at play. Some employees wanted to bunk with their friend at work, others were fine being randomly matched. Sometimes Jim wanted to bunk with Bill, but Bill wanted to bunk with Jerry. Random pairings had to respect gender. The coordination of it all was a people intensive process.

One day, I was standing in the shower, and it just hit me: the whole solution, right in front of me. I went into the office and called a meeting with my team to explain it. Even the cynics on my team were convinced. While in the shower, I'd solved a problem our whole industry had struggled with. My solution would allow attendees to resolve their own issues via clicking special links in emails that triggered behaviors in our systems. It sounds almost too quaint today but back in the early 2000s, it was revolutionary.

I was able to think about work in the shower because I was well-rested with a good work-life balance. It was something I insisted on for my team also. Imagine instead that I'd just finished working my seventh twelve-hour day in a row. My shower time would be zombie-like, with me just welcoming any moment not to think about work. Sure, my company might be getting lots of productivity out of me, but they would likely be getting a lot of mistakes, too, and *no innovation*.

Since that epiphany, I've called ensuring good work-life balance "protecting my teams' shower time." It pays off in spades.

The phrase "burning out" perfectly describes the extinguishing of the flame of creativity and innovation in your employees. Remember that when you tell your teams to go on a death march towards a deadline. You're increasing the chance of mistakes and reducing the chance they will innovate.

Fear of Failure

3M is said to have a database for failed experiments. It is this database that contained the failed experiment for a super adhesive glue. Later, a different 3M employee noticed that people were taping pieces of paper everywhere and wondered if he could develop a glue that was just sticky enough to hold the paper in place. He tried many variations until he consulted the database and found the failed experiment for the super strong glue. The failure in the original context led to the invention of one of the most ubiquitous office supplies known to mankind: the sticky note. It's only because 3M values failure—they created an entire database to capture it—that they were able to benefit from it later. It's also why 3M employees feel safe to fail.

Brené Brown reminds us in her audio course *The Power of Vulnerability* that to innovate is to be vulnerable. Innovation is creating something that has never been created before—which is one of the most vulnerable things a person can do, because not all innovations work out as intended. If a company punishes or frowns upon failure, one of the first casualties is innovation. If employees don't feel safe to try things, they will keep their creative ideas to themselves—or worse, take them to your competitors.

Creating safety to fail means celebrating failure. One European leader I know used to have a segment in his all-hands meetings where he asked teams to talk about something that went wrong that month. One by one, teams would reveal things: "We had a system failure in Belgium last week and we estimate it cost us about thirty minutes of sales. It's making us take a hard look at the health of the system." Following the announcement, the whole group would give raucous applause. It wasn't mockery. They were celebrating the discovery of a weakness in their system.

Too many leaders squander these moments. They spend their all-hands time having teams take turns bragging about what they accomplished rather than what they failed at and learned from.

Brain Drain

A costly withdrawal of innovation is inevitable when the employees with the tribal knowledge and institutional experience leave your company. Yes, new people can bring fresh perspectives, but it would be a mistake to conclude that this is the way to innovate. In fact, it's often a mix of the fresh perspective from a newcomer paired with institutional wisdom from existing employees that can quickly bring ideas to life.

We must reject Jeff Bezos's limiting belief that longtime employees are an albatross upon the neck of innovation. Instead, we want to create an environment that encourages existing employees to experiment. These employees may have an inner roadmap to how things work that took years to build. The innovations they create are based upon all the things that don't work in the current system or are improvements on parts of it that only a veteran would spot. The only way these long-time employees can become an obstacle to innovation is *if you lead them to believe innovating is dangerous for their ego or career*. That creates self-preservation-focused cynics who argue for the status quo.

Brain drain comes into play badly for companies that lean heavily on contractors. Companies that have high turnover or churn through contractors become "forgetting organizations" rather than "learning organizations."[25] All the lessons learned through failure (the most valuable part) walks out the door and goes to another company, aiding that company and forcing yours to relearn them. After all, expertise is not just knowing what to do, it's also knowing what *not* to do. That knowledge comes from trying and failing. You might think that Michael Jordan is very talented, but I suspect he'd be offended by that word. Jordan has practiced *a lot*. He knows more ways that don't work than his opponents do. That's what made him such a great player.

Calculating the Cost

The actual cost of losing your most innovative employees to your competitors or losing the innovative impulses from the ones who stay is going to vary widely from company to company, so I can't provide a formula for your balance sheet. What I hope we

---

[25] A good friend and excellent coach I know named Joel Riddle says it bluntly: "Over-leveraging contractors and not paying attention to turnover is a great way to make your organization collectively dumber."

can agree on, however, is that the cost is significant. It's a cost of lost future revenue in addition to the turnover expenses we discussed earlier. For many businesses, at certain key moments, a failure to innovate means certain doom.

The existence of the problem is further hidden by our acquisition culture. Some companies have made so much money on their initial innovations that they can afford to buy their innovative competitors rather than keeping the fires burning for their own employees. But being chained to their parent company's culture extinguishes the acquired talent's fires all too soon—and the cycle repeats.

Startups know that innovation is their life blood. It's my hope that companies past this stage remember how important it is before it's too late.

Chapter 8: Loss of Agility

agile[26]:
1. *Marked by ready ability to move with quick, easy grace.*
2. *Having a quick, resourceful, and adaptable character.*

---

[26] *Merriam-Webster.com Dictionary*, s.v. "agile," accessed August 16, 2021, https://www.merriam-webster.com/dictionary/agile.

Having spent the better part of the last decade as an Agile Coach, I can tell you that there is no term in modern business that is more misunderstood and misused than the word "agile." For the purposes of our discussion, it's important that I make a distinction between *agile* lowercase and *Agile* uppercase. When I capitalize the word, I mean the Agile framework and all that comes along with it, including the Agile mindset, Scrum, Kanban, Lean, XP, and all the rest. When I lowercase it, I'm referring to the Merriam-Webster definition in this chapter's opening quote. Both usages are relevant to our discussion about the cost of bad leadership; I just want to make sure you understand the distinction.

One important thing to know about uppercase Agile is that it's trying to make your company lowercase agile. Too many leaders treat Agile as if implementing a framework *is the goal*—and as if that goal is for the teams only. These leaders may support coaches who are successful at getting the company's teams to be Agile, but they fail to shift their own mindset around the work those teams do. As a result, the company continues to react just as slowly—sometimes even more slowly than before.

This is not a book about how to pull off a successful Agile transformation, but you can think of it as the prerequisite to being able to do that. If you have an organizational structure and incentives that support a toxic leadership environment, you may be able to check the box for uppercase Agility, but you can forget about the Webster version. If being nimble as a company wasn't your goal at the beginning the transformation, what was?

In case it isn't obvious, only companies that can respond rapidly will survive and flourish. How many companies do you think had COVID on their five-year roadmaps in 2018? The ones who survived were able to pivot very quickly. Consider how drastically and immediately COVID impacted every facet of people's lives—both as consumers and as employees. Companies that spend an inordinate amount of time planning and creating long-range roadmaps are completely wasting the time of many employees—some of them highly paid.

This isn't an argument for no roadmap; having some idea of where you'd like to see the company go in the future is helpful. But too many companies make the mistake of thinking the roadmap is meant to be the trip's agenda. It should be more akin to a list of destinations you'd like to visit than a day-by-day playbook with routes and arrival times. Time (money) you spend on those details is likely wasted. If not COVID, some other disruptive geopolitical or economic force—or just plain competition—is likely waiting in the wings to force you to adapt quickly. Smart leaders know this, which is why many of them jump on the Agile bandwagon, but, again, the mistake they make is assuming Agile is only for their teams and not for them.

I am frequently hired to "get our teams to be Agile." Yes, I can do that. Then at some point, we'll inevitably reach the point where the thing keeping the company from being agile is the leadership team's reluctance to change. So, in this chapter we're going to dive into how leaders often prevent agility *and* Agility at their company—to everyone's detriment.

Contributing to Churn

As we've discussed, bad leaders—or companies with them—have high turnover. That high turnover slows teams down. Teams are constantly trying to recover from the loss of talented team members by stumbling through the work those team members did proficiently. They are also distracted by interviewing candidates to replace lost team members. If done well, that is a huge time sink.

Another way that team instability shows up is in constant reorganization of the company. It seems like every time a new leader is hired or promoted, there is some unspoken rule that the previous leader's structure is *the* problem to solve. This means when leaders change often, structures change often. These reorganizations throw all affected teams back to the *forming* stage of the Tuckman model.

If there are layoffs involved, the rumors and subsequent anxiety will paralyze and distract *everyone* for months. Those left behind will reel from the loss of their coworkers and friends, the increased workload, and the "survivor's guilt."

If team and organizational stability isn't your top priority, it should be. Unstable teams and companies are ineffective at delivering value. It's difficult for teams to be agile when they are always in a state of catch-up.

Churn isn't just unstable teams, it's also unstable backlogs. I'm not talking about the kinds of change in priorities that are driven by market pressures or pandemics. I'm talking about the self-inflicted wounds of office politics, indecisiveness, disinterest, or disengagement. Toxic leaders do not see it as their job to smooth waves of chaos for their teams. They either shift priorities like the wind or create competing priorities for teams who are dependent upon each other. The confusion makes teams feel unsure of what the real priorities are, making it difficult for them to work effectively and autonomously.

How this hampers agility: It's very difficult for a company to be agile about things they *can't control* when they're so busy changing up all the things they *can control*.

Avoiding Accountability

Some years ago, I came out of the front door of my house and saw my neighbor loading something into his car. I said, "Hi Jim!" and scared the living crap out of the man. I think he jumped three feet into the air. Seeing how I'd startled him, I apologized for scaring him. He replied, "No, it's my fault. I should have been more aware of my surroundings."

I've never forgotten that. Here's a man who could have just as easily replied, "Oh it's fine. It happens." Instead, he looked for a way he could be accountable for something.

At the time, I happened to be working for a company where the CEO was a former third string quarterback for a major NFL team. He was on the team when they won a Superbowl, so he had a giant Superbowl ring—which looked ridiculous on his bony hands. Working for this man, I noticed a troubling trend. Whenever one of our teams did great, he was quick to take the credit. Whenever they did poorly, he was quick to blame someone below him. Interesting behavior from the player on the football field who is supposed to lead their team. *Maybe that's why he was rarely on the field*, I thought.

I contrasted his behavior to my neighbor's and realized that the people looking for power the most tend to give it all away the moment they could claim it. After all, if I'm a victim to everyone else's actions, there's nothing I can do. I'm . . . wait for it . . . powerless. Yet if, as my neighbor did, we look for something *we could have done differently*, we claim some or all the power for ourselves to change outcomes in the future.

So many poor leaders I've worked with have long lists of things they hold others accountable for but struggle to even name, let alone take responsibility for, the things the organization is counting on *them* to do. One of those is the care of those who are in their charge.

How this hampers agility: When leaders are quick to point fingers, moving fast is riskier than going slow. If it's not safe to fail, it's not safe to go fast—and slow teams can't be agile.

Kissing Up and Hitting Down

In a similar vein, some leaders, typically Peacock and Ladder Climber archetypes, are known for being very good at caring for those above them even when it means throwing their teams under the bus. This creates a lot of distrust towards that leader and creates a selfish atmosphere. Knowing their boss doesn't have their back, team members begin focusing on their individual goals rather than their team's or the company's goals. It's every person for themselves.

How this hampers agility: Being agile requires that team members pulse to the same rhythm, not to their own individual beats. Many of the Agile principles are rooted in teamwork, trust, and autonomy for this very reason.

Distrusting Employees

Trust issues can go the other way too. When leaders distrust their employees to get the job done, they increase the amount of control over them. They create approval gates that the teams' work must pass through. They tell the teams how to organize and how to work rather than supporting the way the teams agree to work. They dictate who is on teams and appoint outside people they *already* trust into leadership positions rather than promoting from within. This creates an "us and them" atmosphere between leaders and their employees. Distrust is central to all team dysfunction, and it certainly drives the worst behaviors of leadership—command-and-control and micromanagement being two of the most common.

How this hampers agility: With tight control over teams, leaders create approval bottlenecks and other micromanagement tactics that slow teams down.

DEEPER DIVE

The Five Dysfunctions of a Team by Patrick Lencioni

Death Marches

A death march is when a team is told they must meet a fixed deadline with a fixed scope of work. The only thing not fixed is the number of hours employees will have to work to meet it. At the end of these marches, employees are exhausted and demotivated. The quality of the work is usually substandard, leading to a second death march to fix all the mistakes. Then the employees crash and productivity drops to nearly zero for a time. This makes everyone fall behind and sets up the organization for another death march in an endless cycle.

    This cycle is a key contributor to employee disengagement, loss of innovation (see Burnout on page 83), and turnover. Not to mention, it is a major cause of quality issues, which can lead to customer dissatisfaction as well.

How this hampers agility: One of the most important Agile principles says that all processes should "promote sustainable development. The sponsors, developers, and users should be able to maintain a constant pace indefinitely." The quality and disengagement issues that are symptomatic of death marches work against everything a company needs to be able to pivot quickly.

Even if you think the sole purpose of your company is to make money, the ability of the organization to pivot quickly will greatly improve the prospects of capitalizing on market, political, and societal shifts faster than your competition. This is the hope companies have for Agile. But they will never be agile if their leadership team, deliberately or accidentally, behaves in the ways I outlined in this chapter.

Chapter 9: Taking Poison Home

> *Today, many businesses have a toxic influence on the well-being of their team members and their families. We lament what is happening to the youth of the world, yet we in business persist in sending people home broken, and there they struggle with their marriages and with parenting. Many leaders think that people should be grateful and happy simply because they have a job. But the stark fact is that **the way we treat people at work affects the way they feel and how they treat people in their life**. We subject people to our leadership, good and bad, for 40 hours a week, and when they go home, it affects the way they treat others.*

– Bob Chapman & Raj Sisodia[27] (emphasis added)

> *According to the Mayo Clinic, the person you report to at work is more important for your health than your family doctor.*

– Bob Chapman

---

[27] Bob Chapman and Rajendra Sisodia, *Everybody Matters: The Extraordinary Power of Caring for Your People like Family* (New York, NY: Portfolio/Penguin, 2015), [Page 91].

As if you don't already have enough pressure as a leader, here I am telling you that you play a large role in the physical and mental health of your employees and, by extension, society. I wish that assertion was wrong. I so want that to be hyperbole. But it's not. I think deep down we know this is true because of our own experiences. We have a bad day at the office, then we come home and snap at the kids or our spouses because we're "not in the mood."

Leaders create an environment for employees. When that environment is one of long hours, dicey politics, high stress deadlines, and unfulfilling work, it is naïve to think that won't carry over into the home lives of our employees. We simply cannot avoid it.

I do want to make a distinction between *accountable* and *responsible* here. I'm not saying that toxic leaders are responsible for the bad things that happen in their employees' lives and those of their children. I am saying they are greatly accountable for it though. Is that tough to read? Perhaps you are thinking, *No way. I'm not taking that on. How people behave outside their work hours is way outside the scope of what I'm willing to own.*

I don't blame you for thinking that, and you are correct that you don't need to own the behavior of employees after work. Although that does beg the question about why companies drug test employees before hiring them, but I digress. It is time we started looking hard at the connection between the work environments we're creating and the kind of societies we are creating across generations.

We all have a vested interest in getting this right. We all live and function in the societies we're cocreating. High rates of mental and physical illness, crime, and poverty affect us all outside of work. If our working environments have a large direct or indirect impact on these, and those environments are largely controlled by our leadership teams, wouldn't it be good to know that?

The Health Connection

I had just left the doctor after being told that a mysterious skin pain on my side was likely stress related. After the full suite of tests to rule out any of the big nerve-related disorders, my doctor had finally asked if work was stressful.

"Yes, very much, actually. My boss is a jerk and I'm fairly certain it's clinical in his case," I replied.

He said, "Mr. Lemson, I'm really wondering if you're suffering from a stress-related injury here. The nervous system is vulnerable when we're under stress." He suggested some traditional relaxation techniques such as meditation and that I consider taking some time off. He said he would give me a note for work if I needed it. I told him I'd take him up on it if the boss wouldn't give me the time off.

A coach that I was working with at the time had told me, "Sean, the next time your boss screams at you, go for a walk before responding." He explained that it would give me a chance to settle down and respond from the front of my brain rather than the amygdala.

It didn't take long for me to put both my coach's technique and my doctor's diagnosis to the test. I walked into the office a few days later to find my boss berating one of my employees. He seemed to be accusing him of causing a bug. I listened for a moment, then calmly interjected that it would be impossible for his accusation to be true as this employee didn't even have access to the part of the code that would have caused this problem. My boss looked right at me, pointed his finger at my face, and screamed, "You shut up!"

It seemed like a great time to try out that exercise my coach had suggested.

"I'm going for a walk," I announced matter-of-factly and headed for the door.

My boss hollered after me, "Keep walking. You're fired!"

That turned out to be one of the best days of my life. Just a few weeks later, my side pain vanished.

Stress at work comes from high job demands, inflexible working hours, poor job control, poor work design and structure, bullying, harassment, and job insecurity. These stressors, known as psychosocial stressors, are the ones with the most solid connections to stress as it manifests itself in the human body through the secretion of the hormone cortisol. Cortisol is the body's alarm system. It's meant to heighten our survival awareness. Crucial systems in our bodies are regulated through cortisol such as the digestive, reproductive, and immune systems. It manages how the body uses carbohydrates, reduces inflammation, regulates blood pressure, increases blood sugar, controls the sleep/wake cycle, and boosts energy so we can handle the stress that triggered it while restoring balance afterward.

With cortisol, our bodies make a trade. We spot a leopard stalking us, and cortisol trades future days for the possibility of living to see another one in the first place. Key systems in our bodies begin functioning differently in the presence of cortisol, all in the interest of conserving energy and rechanneling it towards behavior that will help us survive. We could have been hungry in the moment before that leopard appeared, but we will suddenly not notice it. If we were tired, we will suddenly be quite awake. If our blood sugar was low, the body will begin converting fat into glucose.

The cost of these systems being ignored and the stress on our cardiovascular system of increased blood pressure and heart rate is a small price to pay if it allows us to escape being leopard food. But it was never meant to be a constant in our system, and if it's present in large periods of our waking moments, it negatively impacts our physical health. It is literally killing us slowly.

When we're under prolonged high stress, we are at an increased chance to develop diabetes, obesity, high cholesterol, high blood pressure, immune deficiency disorders, and gastrointestinal disorders, such as irritable bowel syndrome. We're also more likely to suffer a heart attack or stroke.

My experience with that particularly toxic boss was a big wakeup call for just how insidious this damaging stress is. It truly was a "frog in boiling water" scenario for me. Looking back on those years, I can clearly see how mentally and physically damaging it was to work for my toxic boss, but while I was in "the moment" I had no idea my body was being physically affected and my mental health—primarily my self-esteem—was being pummeled regularly. I wasn't being paid all that well, but it wouldn't have made a difference if I were. It just would have placed a heavier set of golden handcuffs on me to stay and tolerate the abuse.

In America specifically, paid vacations are often rare, so workers rarely get enough space from their jobs to notice these kinds of stresses by feeling their absence. When we do get some time off, it's often not long enough and comes with a pile of work upon our return. We may even do some of that work during our time off to try to keep it manageable when we return. In fact, the entire quiet quitting movement is labor's response to this untenable situation. It's a poorly named description for the behavior of doing exactly what you're paid for and nothing else. It should be titled "doing your job" but because companies are so used to getting that extra work for free, when workers stop doing it, they are suddenly labeled as "quiet quitters." And IRS and Labor Department rules about exempt employees (those exempt from overtime pay) make the situation even worse—essentially legalizing wage theft at many companies.

The Healthcare Connection

As an ironic twist, in America we're chained to the cause of our stress-related illnesses so that we can get treated for them. Healthcare insurance is incredibly expensive here. As a self-employed individual, I pay over $1,200 per month for health insurance for my partner and myself—and that doesn't even include dental or vision. I know people who won't leave their stress-filled jobs because they have families who are dependent on the healthcare insurance provided by their employers. I often wonder how many great entrepreneurial ideas we never get to see because of this stifling situation.

Some have made the very valid argument that this is why companies often lobby against universal healthcare. If everyone suddenly had healthcare as a universal right, that would unlock the figurative handcuffs that hold so many employees hostage at these companies.

The Societal Connection

While reading the book *Everybody Matters* by Bob Chapman, I was struck by the connection he makes, as the CEO of a billion-dollar company, to his responsibility for society at large. Chapman describes the moment he had this epiphany when attending a wedding. As the bride was escorted down the aisle by her father to her future husband, he suddenly realized that every employee in his company was someone's son or daughter. He wanted to treat his employees the way he'd want his own children treated by their companies and bosses. It was a visceral experience he's never been able to shake, and it forms the "why" behind many of his own leadership behaviors and those of the leaders he mentors. He clearly understands that the work environment he and his leaders create directly impacts the families of the employees who work within it.

Chapman's story reminds us that all companies and their leaders directly and indirectly impact society. If we underpay our employees, we create hardship for their families—both physical and mental. We make it harder for them to purchase nutritional food or to put their kids through college. If we create a cutthroat environment where everyone puts in extra hours to keep their jobs, we make it harder for employees to find time to cook, help their children with homework, go to softball games and school plays, or help elderly parents. We keep them "always on" and that keeps them from ever really getting the downtime they need to recharge. These stressed-out employees then often take it out on their families with shorter attention spans and fuses. This can contribute to divorces among married couples.

According to various studies, the top reasons for divorce are listed below in order. As you read the list, try to think about which might be greatly influenced by stress at work caused by a terrible leader, boss, or company:

1. Too much conflict, incessant arguing
2. Lack of commitment
3. Infidelity/extramarital affairs
4. Lack of emotional and/or physical intimacy
5. Communication problems between partners
6. Domestic violence
7. Opposing values or morals
8. Addiction (alcohol, drugs, gambling, or sex)
9. Absence of romantic intimacy or love
10. One spouse not carrying their weight in the marriage
11. Financial problems and debt

Some of the same behaviors that destroy marriages can lead to entire generations of kids being raised without attentive parents. Many of these kids act out and turn to unhealthy ways to get attention, which are often detrimental to their own lives and sometimes detrimental to society at large. From 1980 to 1989, the median age of mass shooters was thirty-nine. Since 2020, it is now just twenty-two years old—mostly young men and boys. Even if you don't have a spouse or children, you are living in the world we are collectively creating.

Before I'm taken entirely out of context and accused of blaming mass shootings on bad leaders, let me be clear that I'm not suggesting this direct link. There is strong evidence, however, that the way we raise our children during crucial points in their development has a direct impact on the emotional health of those children. According to the CDC:

> One in 14 children aged 0–17 years had a parent who reported poor mental health, and those children were more likely to have poor general health, to have a mental, emotional, or developmental disability, to have adverse childhood experiences such as exposure to

violence or family disruptions including divorce, and to be living in poverty.²⁸

Another study conducted by the University of South Carolina found that the children of adults who reported high parenting stress were three times more likely to experience four or more adverse childhood experiences (ACEs). Numerous studies have concluded that parents who have been exposed to ACEs are more likely to expose their own children to ACEs, making this a vicious cycle. Effects of ACEs may be long-term, with poorer mental, physical, and behavioral outcomes in adulthood. They also lead to a heightened propensity for various chronic conditions such as diabetes, heart disease, cancer, and depression. Again this study concludes:

> Repeated and unmitigated exposure to adverse events during childhood may activate stress-related hormones in the brain, which may lead to toxic stress and the disruption of healthy brain development in children and adolescents.²⁹

I could cite more and more studies that have all reached similar conclusions, but I don't think it's a huge leap of faith to conclude that if workers are stressed out and they are unable to shield their growing children from that stress, it affects the development of those children's brains. This can cause mental health issues for those children when they reach adolescence. It isn't hard to imagine the various ways these issues manifest themselves in society as these adolescents grow into adulthood. Many learn to adapt—some do not.

---

[28] U.S. Department of Health and Human Services, "Mental Health of Children and Parents—A Strong Connection," Centers for Disease Control and Prevention, last modified March 8, 2023, accessed August 28, 2023, https://www.cdc.gov/childrensmentalhealth/features/mental-health-children-and-parents.html.

[29] Elizabeth Crouch et al., "Exploring the Association between Parenting Stress and a Child's Exposure to Adverse Childhood Experiences (ACEs)," *Children and Youth Services Review* 102 (July 2019), accessed November 15, 2023, https://doi.org/10.1016/j.childyouth.2019.05.019.

An Existential Crisis

Corporations and leaders have gotten a free pass up to now on the accountability they have for their part of the chain of events that lead to societal issues. But I think that free pass is unwarranted. Remember, companies are active participants in the government. They have massive lobbying machinery and use it to successfully manipulate lawmakers and overpower viewpoints they don't agree with. They don't get to participate at that level of society and then throw their hands up when the societal outcomes of these policies are destructive.

This disowning is made easier by euphemisms and obscurity. After all, leadership is easy when we don't trouble ourselves to consider that those we lead are human beings. Most companies create a dehumanizing model to help with the hard parts of leadership: deciding wages, coaching low performers, staff sizing, handling low employee engagement, balancing shareholder value with long-term viability. Those tough challenges are made much easier when we convince ourselves that those affected are headcount, resources, or human capital. These euphemisms for human beings allow us to mistreat them and let ourselves off the hook for the parts we directly affect but don't want to own.

Ultimately, this is an existential crisis for capitalism and for corporations operating inside of it. Twenty-first century leadership must include a recognition of humanity. We can no longer turn people (or the planet, for that matter) into numbers and dollar signs. If we fail to do this, we should not be surprised when society erodes to the point that there no longer is a market to operate inside of.

DEEPER DIVE

Dying for a Paycheck by Jeffrey Pfeifer
Corporate Bullsh*t: Exposing the Lies and Half-Truths That Protect Profit, Power, and Wealth in America by Nick Hanauer

---

PART THREE

BECOMING A BETTER LEADER

We need to get all those managers who believe they finished their education at graduation to understand that they are at risk of becoming more finished than educated.

– Bjarte Bogsnes, author of *Implementing Beyond Budgeting: Unlocking the Performance Potential*

Chapter 10: Your Mindset About Leadership

The first principle is that you must not fool yourself—and you are the easiest person to fool.

– Richard Feynman

The word "mindset" is thrown about quite often these days. What exactly is a mindset? How did we get one? How do we change it? What impact does it have on our daily lives? Why is it important to understand this in a leadership book?

Put succinctly, we behave in ways that make sense to us, and what makes sense to us is encapsulated in our mindset. All the leaders who behave in the toxic ways we've discussed thus far are doing what makes sense to them. All of us have mindsets that influence our behavior—even when that behavior is unproductive or flat out wrong. As an extreme example, even serial killers are doing what makes sense to *them*.

It follows, then, that if we want to change our behaviors in the long term, we have to change our mindsets.

There is a bit of a chicken and egg debate in the professional business coaching world. Some believe that you change minds by changing behaviors and others believe you change behaviors by changing minds. I think the real answer is in between. Yes, clearly you can change minds by changing behaviors—this is especially true about people with fixed mindsets[30] who fear anything they think they'll struggle with. Sometimes just trying something and seeing it work can change a mind. However, *lasting* change requires a change in mindset at some point. Some can start at the mind and others just need to behave their way into the change (usually kicking and screaming as they go). As a coach, I usually begin with the mind since it can create such powerful obstacles to behavior, and I only do the behavioral work with the stubborn holdouts.

What *is* a mindset, exactly? I define it as a collection of values, beliefs, and principles. Let's examine each one individually.

---

[30] We'll cover growth and fixed mindsets in Chapter 11, but for now think of a growth mindset as someone who welcomes growth through learning and a fixed as someone who steers clear of things they aren't already good at or think they wouldn't be good at.

Values

Values are comparative in nature. When you talk about something you hold dear, you're talking about a value—even if the thing you're comparing it against isn't mentioned. For example, if you value peace and quiet, you value it *more* than busy distractions. You may value telling the truth (over feeling comfortable), alone time (over being around others), spending time with your kids (over other activities), making money (over doing work you enjoy).

In my coaching practice, values are a big part of the process I use with clients. Values are like a compass and a map to help us navigate tough life choices. When we act in accordance with our values, we feel "right" and when we act out of accordance with them, we feel unfulfilled, depressed, unsettled, or dissatisfied.

Values are usually reached by experimentation. We tried something and learned that we liked it, or we learned we didn't like it and began valuing its opposite. We aren't born with our values; we decide on them as life happens around us. The older we get, the less we tend to reevaluate our values and the firmer we feel about them. That isn't necessarily a good thing because it can make us too rigid for a changing world.

Beliefs

Beliefs are things we can't prove but believe anyway. They're often captured in short phrases we say to ourselves and others. A few examples I've heard as I've coached people to change their behaviors are below. I'm not presenting any of these as true or false; I'm just listing beliefs I've heard from others. As you read these beliefs, try to imagine a few behaviors of someone that would hold them:

- There's never a cop around when you need one.
- People work harder when they have a deadline. (Corollary: People are lazy unless they have a deadline.)
- Honesty is the best policy.
- You never forget the truth.

- What comes around, goes around.
- People who are successful have worked hard to get it. (Corollary: People who are unsuccessful are lazy.)
- Nice guys finish last.
- Sometimes you have to cheat/lie to win.
- Winning is everything.
- Women are more emotional than men.
- Real men don't cry.
- Kids should be seen not heard.
- Video games make kids violent.
- Salespeople can't be trusted.

Critical thinkers are quick to change beliefs if new evidence emerges. They care more about *getting it right* than they do about *being right*. Others tend to form their beliefs emotionally and hold them regardless of disconfirming evidence. They care more about *being right* than *getting it right*. This is one of the nasty places where confirmation bias raises its head. If we believe something is true, we're likely to avoid or downplay evidence that disproves it and see (and even exaggerate) the evidence that supports it.

All of us are walking around with beliefs like these in our heads that greatly impact our behavior. In addition to forming our own beliefs based on our firsthand experiences, we may have adopted beliefs from others growing up without ever challenging them. Racism, homophobia, and bigotry can begin this way.

DEEPER DIVE

Think Again by Adam Grant

Principles

Principles are like a summary of a value and belief captured in a bold statement that usually has an air of "always" or "never." For example:

- **"I always tell the truth."**
    - Honors beliefs: "Honesty is the best policy" and "You never forget the truth."
    - Honors value: "I value telling the truth over feeling comfortable."
- **"I (always) treat people the way I want to be treated."**
    - Honors belief: "What comes around, goes around."
    - Honors value: "I value fairness over getting my way."

Principles usually follow deep life lessons. If someone close to us betrayed us, for example, we may have a principle around trust resulting from that betrayal. Because principles stand atop values and beliefs, they usually only change when the underlying values and/or beliefs change.

Just like principles are the result of values and beliefs, behaviors are a result of our mindset. If our actions make sense to us but we don't like the results we're getting, the place to look is at our mindset.

Appendix A has a worksheet to help you figure out your mindset about leadership. Once you identify your values, beliefs, and principles, you will clearly see how your current behaviors line up—or you'll realize that you're behaving out of alignment with a value you already have. Either way, I've found that examining values and beliefs is the best way to modify behavior.

Feeling right isn't the same as *being* right. Feeling right just means we're behaving in accordance with our mindset. Being right involves many other facets: facts, laws, outcomes, morals, obligations, and circumstances among many others. What you're doing as a leader may *feel* right but if your turnover is high or engagement scores are low, maybe you're wrong anyway. If you're paying attention, you can spot when your mindset isn't serving you. These are usually big "aha!" moments in our lives. I've witnessed these in my clients from just having them list out their beliefs. They realize that they adopted a belief from a parent that, upon examination, just isn't true. Once they let go of that belief, they free themselves to reexamine their values, and as soon as they do, their old principles change or fall away. The behavior changes next.

A change like this one is usually very fast and permanent. The whole process is simple but not easy, yet it's a crucial ability if you're going to change the leader that you are.

Motives: A Mindset in Practice

> As it turns out, the primary motive for most young people, and too many older ones, is the rewards that leadership brings with it. Things like notoriety, status, and power. But people who are motivated by these things won't embrace the demands of leadership when they see little or no connection between doing their duties and receiving those rewards. They'll pick and choose how they spend their time and energy based on what they are going to get, rather than what they need to give to the people they are supposed to be leading.
>
> – Patrick Lencioni, Author of *The Motive*

The quote above is taken from the book *The Motive* by Patrick Lencioni. In a podcast interview about the book, he said that while it was his most recent of many books, he wished he'd written it first because it's so fundamental to good leadership.

Motive is the strategic "why" behind our actions. It's the root word of "motivation." We are motivated to achieve outcomes that align with our mindset, so we set out to bring those outcomes to reality through our behavior. Lencioni divides leadership motives into two categories:[31]

- *Reward-centered:* The belief that being a leader is the reward for hard work; therefore, the experience of being a leader should be pleasant and enjoyable, free to choose what they work on and avoid anything mundane, unpleasant, or uncomfortable.
- *Responsibility-centered:* The belief that being a leader is a responsibility; therefore, the experience of leading should be difficult and challenging (though certainly not

---

[31] Patrick Lencioni, *The Motive* (Hoboken, NJ: John Wiley & Sons, 2020)

without elements of personal gratification).

Notice how both motive types are defined by their *beliefs*. At the risk of oversimplifying the issue of toxic leadership, reward-centered leaders are almost always toxic to the companies they work for and the employees who work for them. Their pursuit of leadership as a reward means they see leading people as a burden but leadership itself as an achievement. Because reward-centered leaders believe that leadership *is the reward*, they think that achieving higher positions of leadership means getting *more reward*. They spend a lot of their energy figuring out who/what can help them get ahead, who is competing for their next role, and who is just a distraction that needs to be dealt with or ignored (often it's their employees and their issues that land in this last category).

If you are a reward-centered leader, you are part of the problem. If you're reading this book because you want to be a better leader, then my next question will be: *What is your motive?* Because if you're trying to learn the skills of great leadership so you can rise in the ranks merely for the achievement of it, please rethink that.

If, on the other hand, you see leadership as a calling where your skills and abilities at motivating people can benefit a company, then you've got a motive that will fit nicely with the tools I'm presenting here.

Money as a Motive

Since we're discussing motives for leadership, I must mention this here: If you're vying for a promotion into leadership because it's the only way you can make more money at your company, but you don't feel a calling to lead people, you are following a path that won't serve you or your company. There's nothing wrong with wanting to make more money, but if it's your sole or primary motive, you likely won't make a good leader.

The policies and budget decisions that create this bad incentive fall squarely in HR and finance, so we will tackle that in Part 4, but if you're working for a company that doesn't provide the opportunity to make more money without going into leadership, my advice is to find one that has higher-paying individual contributor roles available for you.

Motives in your Culture

It's not good enough that *you* are a responsibility-centered leader—even if you're the CEO. Responsibility-centered leadership must permeate your company's leadership philosophy from top to bottom. A single rewards-centered leader can begin the transformation into an everyone-out-for-themselves rewards-centered culture.

One company I worked with had a CEO who was very mindful of his responsibility. It just oozed from his pores during his all-hands meetings, and I think people genuinely trusted and liked the man. But the further you got from him, the more you saw rewards-centered leadership emerge. One example: The company provided reserved parking spots for leaders right next to the doors. Rather than address the lack of parking for employees, they created a daily reminder that those employees weren't important while indicating to leaders that leadership had its privileges.

But parking spots weren't the only issue. Employees began noticing that leaders who didn't care about the company's mission were being hired from outside. You could read it all over these leaders' faces (and their résumés) that this company was merely a steppingstone in their career aspirations. Those newly-hired leaders then filled a large division of the company's best middle and upper-middle management positions with cronies from their previous companies. This closed the door to committed employees who were vying to be promoted into those positions, short circuiting career paths and spurring many of them to leave.

Lest you think I'm exaggerating, a LinkedIn search for these leaders and their directs would reveal a gang moving through the same companies one after another. One by one the mercenaries would be hired, and the missionaries would leave.

I watched the spirit of an entire company division be . . . well . . . murdered. I know it sounds hyperbolic but saying the spirit *died* doesn't quite capture the intentional disregard for it that led to its death. This group of grifters was rewards-focused. They didn't feel a responsibility to their employees nor to the mission of the company. Their departure was as predictable as their motives were. One would leave at the top, then three to six months later another, then another. Unsurprisingly they'd all end up at the same company again. Each with an exit package, a huge chunk of options, and promotions at their next company while leaving the previous one drained, dispirited, and disorganized. A shadow of what it once was. And, importantly, this all happened under the CEO I mentioned whom everybody genuinely liked. He just apparently didn't think it was his main job to make sure his clear love of the company and his caring nature were protected parts of the culture.

Don't be this company. Hire (or even better, promote) leaders who believe in your just cause and share your respect for the missionaries at the company.

DEEPER DIVE

The Motive by Patrick Lencioni

A Beginner's Mind

The me of today is nothing like the me of fifteen years ago—and I don't just mean the normal stuff. I'm a different person. If you knew me then, you'd probably like the me of today a lot more. The difference is primarily the result of one experience that really stands out. Up to that point, if I'd offended someone with something I said, I would tell myself (and often the offended person) that this was their problem. I had a belief that said that I couldn't over-own their experience. It was their responsibility to own their reaction.

Then, in an intensive leadership program I participated in, I found out just how wrong—and right—I was.

Because of the strength of the connection and the safety that existed between the attendees of this program, we all had many opportunities to tell others how they were landing with us. As you can probably imagine, as people started telling me that I wasn't landing the way I intended, I started out with the ol' "That's your problem" routine. Then I realized the entire group was saying I was landing in a way entirely different than I intended. Could all twenty of them be wrong? At what point did the way I landed become *my* problem?

I soon realized and accepted that my previous belief was about as un-leaderlike as it could be. A leader owns their impact and is continually sensing it, willing to try again if things go differently than intended.

That one learning sent me tumbling. What other beliefs did I hold that were not serving me in catastrophic and far-reaching ways? I had to retrain my ego to be proud of learning new things rather than defending what I already knew. I had to stop pretending that I always had all the answers and start figuring out the questions.

This was my jolt into the beginner's mind. It doesn't require me to pretend not to know things, but it certainly forces me to think again about things I think I know—especially when the results are not what I'm expecting.

That's not the complete story, though. Leaders also control the way they are impacted. During one of our group circle discussions, a soft-spoken woman spoke up and said that she felt that I didn't create any space for her to participate. I remember thinking, *Here we go. I'm about to get a lecture on creating space for others.* One of our tribe leaders looked at her and replied, "When are you going to start *taking* space?" It was a jaw-dropping moment. Up to that moment, most of us had experienced this woman as a quiet—nearly invisible—participant of the group. She went through life being pushed around by people like me. And while there was a learning for me about creating space, this was a turning point for her. For the rest of the program, she honed the skill of politely, but forcefully, owning her space. Incidentally, today she is now a *rock star* consultant. She's written a book, runs her own successful consulting business, and is genuinely a force to be reckoned with.

She and I were both trapped in beliefs that were not serving us. Being willing to challenge those kinds of beliefs is what having a beginner's mind is all about. You get there by shutting down or retraining your ego and avoiding biases based on those flawed beliefs.

To do that, it helps a bit to understand the learning flow that all humans progress through.

The Stages of Learning

Whenever we learn something new, we all go through four stages in sequence:

1. Unconscious incompetence
2. Conscious incompetence
3. Conscious competence
4. Unconscious competence

In the **unconscious incompetence** stage, we don't know what we don't know. Once we become aware of what we don't know, we are in the **conscious incompetence** stage. After we've practiced for a while, we move to the **conscious competence** stage. We can do the task, but we must think about it to do it. When we've been doing it many times or for a long period of time, many of the motions of the task move to our subconscious mind and we reach the **unconscious competence** stage.

It seems simple enough, but (as usual), there's more to it. The Dunning-Kruger effect—a cognitive bias named after David Dunning and Justin Kruger—is where our confidence exceeds our competence. Put simply, we don't know enough about the topic to judge our own skill, knowledge, or ability accurately—so we overestimate it. I've combined several of these ideas together in Figure 4.

Figure 4: The Dunning-Kruger Effect

A graph plotting Confidence (y-axis, 0 to 100) vs. Knowledge (x-axis, Novice to Expert). Key points along the curve:
- "I'll just watch a YouTube video." (Novice, Unconscious Incompetence)
- "Ok I got this. Lemme try to land the plane." — Peak of Mount Ignorance (confidence ~100)
- "Hmm. This is harder than I thought."
- "I'm never going to get this." — Valley of despair (Conscious Incompetence)
- "Ok I'm starting to get it now." (Conscious Competence)
- "Trust me, it's complicated." (Expert, Unconscious Competence)
- Imposter Syndrome branch continues flat from the valley to the right.

You'll notice in the graph that when people push past their initial overconfidence, things look very scary for a while. This is the moment that many people quit. They drop out of college, change majors, or make excuses for why they don't need to know this. Anything to escape the valley of despair where our saboteurs are telling us we're not smart enough, not young enough, not old enough, not attractive enough, not extroverted enough, not . . . enough. It's only when we continue to persevere at this junction that we can begin to really excel in our knowledge and turn it into wisdom.

    Some continue past this junction and grow their knowledge, but their confidence never seems to rise again. This is the beginning of imposter syndrome—when our competence exceeds our confidence. Imposter syndrome is complicated because it's a function of your upbringing, the people you surround yourself with, and whether you have a growth or fixed mindset about your work—a topic we'll revisit in more detail in the next chapter. Imposter syndrome is a big deal with leadership. According to multiple studies:[32]

- 70 percent of successful people reported experiencing imposter feelings at some point in their life.
- 80 percent of CEOs feel out of their depth in their role.
- 84 percent of entrepreneurs and small business owners report experiencing imposter syndrome.

Dozens of books have been written about the topic, so I won't spend a lot of time on it here other than to show the place along the learning process that we tend to go down that path. Understanding all of this can help you navigate the journey of learning something new. At the outset, when the temptation to think "I got this" is strong, you can remind yourself that there's much more to learn, young Jedi. When you're sitting in the valley of despair, and it's tempting to think you're dumb or incapable of "getting it," you can remind yourself that many people get stuck in that spot and that perseverance is the ticket out.

I realize that my readers come from all levels of experience in leadership. One thing I know to be true is that whatever your current mindset is about leadership, you cannot change it without at least bringing your mind back to a place of believing there is something for you to learn. This will be even more important if you've been doing the job for a while. But, as the Dunning-Kruger effect demonstrates, both new and experienced leaders can get stuck on the peak of Mount Ignorance. That too will prevent learning.

---

[32] Imposter Syndrome Institute, "You're Not Alone," Imposter Syndrome Institute, last modified 2023, accessed January 21, 2023, https://impostorsyndrome.com/infographics/youre-not-alone/.

To conquer what's coming in the book, it's important that you develop a beginner's mind. Here's how I define this mentality:

- You are willing to challenge existing beliefs and values—even deeply held ones.
- You do not need to be the smartest person in the room. You care more about getting it right than being right.
- You are deeply curious (a mental state of wanting to know more) and inquisitive (asking questions of others—curiosity in action).
- You listen to understand, not to respond.

A beginner's mind is one that is hypervigilant at watching for biases and beliefs trying to shut down growth or preserve existing understandings (usually to save the ego). If those with a beginner's mind have an ego about anything, it's that they take pride in wanting to *know more* rather than in thinking they *know everything* there is to know. Let's explore the four components of a beginner's mind.

Challenging Existing Beliefs and Assumptions

Challenging your existing beliefs and assumptions means going beyond having an open mind. It means *actively seeking out* counterpoints to a belief. If you have a deeply held belief that people only get things done when they have a deadline, run some experiments to challenge that belief. Actively seek people out who hold a different belief and have a conversation with them about it.

While you're having that conversation . . .

Release the Need to Be the Smartest Person in the Room

The ego is a powerful mechanism of the mind. When it's employed to protect what we already think is true, it is a formidable obstacle to having one's mind changed. For some, this is literally a biochemical life-or-death situation. When others present a differing opinion, it may as well be a leopard leaping out of a bush. This works against us because some of the smartest people around us simply don't care enough about whether we have it right to fight us over it. They just silently mark us as idiots and move along. What a missed opportunity to grow!

When you disagree with something said, instead of putting out that "death match" vibe about what you think you know, express the beliefs your opinion is based upon and open them up for scrutiny. These can be magical moments of mind-changing. As we discussed earlier, changing just one core belief can lead to many other pieces getting reworked and entire principles falling away. Perhaps that's why the ego fights so hard to prevent it. Don't succumb to the ego. As I mentioned, my trick for this is to try to take the perspective that I'm proud of my open-mindedness and curiosity, not proud of my existing knowledge. That tasks the ego to protect open-mindedness instead of existing opinions.

Remain Deeply Curious and Inquisitive

Curiosity is a mindset and inquisitiveness is an action. I can be curious without asking anything. I can also ask lots of questions and not care about the answers . . . just going through the motions to *appear* curious. We've all seen what this looks like. Someone asks us what we did over the weekend, but they immediately look disinterested or rapidly change the topic to what *they* did over the weekend.

Curiosity also isn't "loaded." It's not "hey, I'm curious… why didn't you take out the trash this morning?" We all know that translates to, "There is no good reason for you not taking the trash out this morning, and this was just my way of bringing it up so I could pounce on you for it."

Curiosity is a yearning for new information and the space created in our mind for it. One of the primary ways we fill that space is through being inquisitive—asking questions—and listening to understand the response.

Listen to Understand

As Tom Yorton, coauthor of the book *Yes, And* describes it, so many people listen to others like they're on a game show. They've got their hands over the buzzer ready to smack it the minute they think they know what the other person is about to say. They've stopped listening at that point and are (sometimes) just waiting to speak.

Listening to understand is different because it's coming from that place of curiosity. There's a hole that must be filled and listening to what the other is saying is the way to fill it. Ironically, there is speaking involved in listening to understand. It usually sounds like, "So what I'm hearing you say is . . ." followed by, "Do I have that right?" You're not building a case for your rebuttal. You're trying to see what the topic looks like from their perspective—discussing the beliefs they hold that make their position feel right to them—and communicating that you're interested in understanding them correctly.

If you genuinely want to change a mindset, you must remove the shackles that your ego has placed on your existing values, beliefs, and principles surrounding that mindset. Most people recognize the futility of fighting someone's ego and are not motivated to try it. How many people with better information have you shut out in this way? How much more successful could you be if you took pride in *getting it right* versus *being right*? The most successful leaders I've worked for and with have found a balance between conviction and curiosity. They can dare to know something while not being at all married to it.

We all admire leaders who can do this, don't we? Why not be one of them?

Empathy Is Required

> *Empathy is really important. Only when our clever brain and our human heart work together in harmony can we achieve our full potential.*
>
> – Jane Goodall

Over the years, I've read *many* books on leadership. A vast majority of them are, in some fashion, telling readers that being a good leader means caring about the people they lead. I've made the argument here myself and will make it several more times before the end of this book. It occurred to me, however, that a significant number of people in leadership positions are *incapable* of doing that. I can't think of one leadership book I've read over the years that has tackled empathy dead on—specifically people's *inability* to have it. Many treat the advice they give as if every reader is just one brilliant point away from an "aha!" moment where they suddenly realize that all that's been missing is caring about others.

As I mentioned before, psychologists generally refer to the lack of ability to feel empathy coupled with a lack of conscience as the primary traits of psychopaths. If a person lacks empathy but still has a conscience, they are generally referred to as a sociopath.[33] Hollywood makes it tempting to assume that all psychopaths and sociopaths are dangerous. That's not true. It's probably more accurate to say that most cold-hearted killers are psychopaths or sociopaths but not all psychopaths and sociopaths are cold-hearted killers. Many are just ruthlessly climbing corporate ladders, manipulating others to get what they want without regard for anyone they perceive to be standing in the way of their goals.

---

[33] Kara Mayer Robinson, "Sociopath v. Psychopath: What's the Difference?" ed. Joseph Goldberg, WebMD, last modified August 24, 2014, accessed December 1, 2021, https://www.webmd.com/mental-health/features/sociopath-psychopath-difference.

One of the most frustrating parts of my job as a leadership coach is when I'm tasked with helping someone who is incapable of empathy to become a better leader. I'm often making the "empathy is needed" case to someone who has been consistently rewarded for their *lack* of empathy up to that point. In too many companies, empathy in leaders is viewed as weakness. If you are instructed to lay off a hundred employees, *your* leaders expect you to be a good soldier and follow orders. It's definitely easier to execute instructions like that if you don't let things like the employees' happiness, satisfaction, survival, physical and mental health, fulfillment, and career progression get in the way. When people come in reminding you of these things, they're annoying, right? Why can't they just let you make the decision to lay off hundreds of employees so we can make our numbers this quarter without reminding you that it's November and that would put everyone out of work right before the holidays?

It's quite easy to manage without empathy. What takes real skill and courage is learning how to face the incredible complexity of the human beings in your charge and balance that against the complexity of corporate obligations and incentives. We've lost our way in these challenging moments. We've forgotten that paying and treating employees well in our own company means having happy paying customers in the market all companies are relying on. We've lost the symbiotic nature of our work. If our customers are nothing but cash-making machines, then our employees are nothing but resources who are to be used up to get us more cash. We've even named the department in charge of handling these people "Human Resources."

Leaders tell employees that they matter, but too often, the people who are promoted to leadership seem to be the ones who can act as if they don't.

Lack of Empathy Is a Drop of Poison

Nothing will frustrate leaders who *have* empathy more than working for a company that doesn't value it. I've witnessed the dance many times in my career. A charismatic, empathic leader will be demoted for speaking up on behalf of employees one too many times at leadership meetings. They resign and are replaced by a "real go-getter" who has a trophy case full of achievements—none of which are first place for any popularity contests. The irony is that the departing leader could have convinced their employees to do just about anything. The new leader just orders people around. Talented employees will rapidly exit the company in response—often to follow the leader who left.

If you are a senior leader in your company and you agree with me that empathy is your secret weapon, your job is to make sure that you never hire or promote a person into a position to lead others who doesn't see eye to eye with you about that and/or who does not possess the capability to experience empathy. Take your eye off that ball and it's only a matter of time before you have allowed your first drop of poison into the company.

If you're one of the estimated 1 percent of people[34] in the world who is incapable of or desensitized to empathy, you are not broadly equipped to be a good leader. There are some realities we must accept. Yes, there are companies who will view your inability to feel for others as a strength. My belief is that companies are rapidly discovering that they'd better stop doing that or no one will stay working for them for long.

If you don't have a capacity for empathy, please climb the individual contributor ladder until you can see other continents. But refrain from taking a job that is responsible for leading others—even if it's offered to you. You'll be making the world a better place.

I'm aware that trying to ask a sociopath to think about others is a bit futile. But sociopaths are usually aware of their lack of ability to feel empathy. They aren't all striving for power and authority, some are just trying to get along in the world. So,

---

[34] Lest you dismiss 1 percent as an insignificant number, at the time of this writing, 1 percent of the world population is 79,539,525 people.

it's possible that I can simply suggest that being a leader is a bad career choice for a sociopath and they will take the advice. But we can't count on it. This only strengthens my point that everyone who is *not* a sociopath needs to remain vigilant that sociopaths do not get into positions of authority or power over others.

> **DEEPER DIVE**
>
> *Corruptible: Who Gets Power and How It Changes Us* by Brian Klaas

CHAPTER 11: YOUR MINDSET ABOUT THE WORK

Good leaders build products. Great leaders build cultures. Good leaders deliver results. Great leaders develop people. Good leaders have vision. Great leaders have values. Good leaders are role models at work. Great leaders are role models in life.

—Adam Grant

In coaching teams and leaders over the past decade, I've discovered that too many of them pay very light attention to some important aspects of work. Being apathetic about or unfamiliar with these concepts is a huge miss. Some of the most transformational moments I've witnessed on teams have occurred after everyone faced these concepts and consciously formed values around them. In this chapter, I'll introduce the concepts and tell you how the best leaders I know use them to drive incredible culture and engagement.

Effectiveness over Efficiency

One of my favorite Agile leaders, Ken Rubin, uses a wonderful analogy to teach the concept of effectiveness versus efficiency. He often says, "Watch the baton, not the runner." In a relay race, it's the first baton crossing the finish line that wins the race, not the team that kept its runners running the most. Rubin says that if we ran relay teams the way we run our businesses, we'd ask the runners who are waiting for the baton to run up and down the bleachers or run another race entirely. That's very efficient but it's not very effective.

Time and time again, leaders make the mistake of maximizing efficiency without considering effectiveness. One of the phrases I hear thrown around organizations is "bias to action," and yet a bias to action can lead to people running around looking busy without impacting what's important. What would it look like if we instead had a bias to *impact*?

If I walk past John's desk and he's reading a magazine, is he being efficient? No. But is he being effective? Perhaps. John could be waiting for a job to finish on the computer and wants to remain ready to jump on the task when it finishes. If he took on a different task for work, he may have to keep going on that new task to get it to a stopping place before he could context switch back to the original task. Again, that would be efficient, but not effective. We've kept John running but the baton from his first race is on the ground waiting for him to finish his second race. Incidentally, the American Psychological Association research on the topic of context switching says it costs us about twenty-three minutes, on average, to regain focus *each time* we switch tasks.

The reason leaders go after efficiency first is because *in*efficiency is easy to spot. We usually must peel back the onion quite a bit to spot ineffectiveness. Like our relay runners, someone sitting idle may look inefficient as an *individual*, but they might be doing the most effective thing for the *team* and for the value the team is delivering.

Resolving *inefficiency* can be as simple as telling John to get back to work or creating metrics to track and ensure people are always moving. Resolving *ineffectiveness* isn't often as easy. We may have to hire or retrain people, examine our workflow, perhaps even reorganize the teams. It's much easier to focus on the quick hit of efficiency, but that is the classic mistake that good leaders avoid.

To be clear, I'm not suggesting that you abandon the pursuit of efficiency. I'm suggesting that you pursue effectiveness *over* efficiency. What good does it do the company for your employees to be efficiently ineffective? Great teams and leaders value effectiveness more than efficiency. Even if that translates to a slower start.

Outcomes over Outputs

In the same way that we're easily tempted to spot and treat efficiency over effectiveness, we're also tempted to fixate on outputs rather than outcomes.

Let's consider our car or phone navigation. It is outcome-focused. The outcome is the address we've indicated we want to get to. The outputs are the numerous streets we'll be turning on to get there. If we miss a turn, the navigation automatically adapts, providing us with a new way to get where we're going. If it instead insisted that we turn around and drive on the street we missed, it would take us much longer to reach our destination. It is this fixation on the *destination* and not on the *route* that makes the tool so adaptable and effective.

Too many leaders fixate on their prescribed solutions rather than where they want to end up. Perhaps they carefully considered the issue and created a plan to address it, so it seems tempting to *follow that plan*. However, to be truly agile, one needs to value *responding to change* over following a plan. This is one of Agile's (capital A) most important values.

This sounds simple, so why do so many leaders get this wrong? I suspect ego is one reason. Many leaders, perhaps rightfully, believe they were promoted into their roles because of their subject matter expertise. As a result, they fall in love with their solution, and they trust themselves more than their employees to solve the problem. The illusion of understanding causes them to overestimate the amount of awareness they have of what's really going on at the frontlines. Consequently, their teams turn into a bunch of disgruntled box checkers, making sure they drive down every road on the plan instead of focusing on the destination.

Leaders must be especially cautious about the tendency to focus on outputs when they ask for metrics. It is very tempting to count the number of streets we drove down to get where we're going, but it would be far more useful to know how close we are to the destination and how long it's taking us to get there. There are uses for output measurement, of course, but leaders tend to *set targets* on these outputs—which is, by far, the worse thing they could do (see Goodhart's Law in Chapter 3). For example, if I want to optimize my navigation to get to our destination faster, setting a target to travel the fewest number of streets or the fewest number of turns is tempting, but it may actually increase the travel time.

Complex vs. Complicated

As we mentioned in our discussion about the Cynefin framework[35] in Chapter 4, there is a huge difference in the way teams and leaders need to show up to face complication versus the way they are called to act when facing complexity. When

---

[35] David J. Snowden and Mary E. Boone, "A Leader's Framework for Decision Making." *Harvard Business Review*, November 2007, accessed October 20, 2021, https://hbr.org/2007/11/a-leaders-framework-for-decision-making.

encountering complication, everyone's job is to sense, analyze, and respond. However, they must probe, sense, and respond to complexity. Complication calls for thoughtful planning; complexity calls for experimentation.

More importantly, leaders' expectations should be different in each circumstance. If a team is facing a complicated problem, it is completely normal for leaders to expect planning, expertise, and tools such as Gannt charts to be used to derive an approximate date for delivery, for example. If that same team is facing a complex problem, expecting a delivery date at the outset of the project is unreasonable (and unfortunately too common).

One of the most common issues I see while coaching organizations is that leaders—often far removed from the actual work—see the problems their teams are solving as complicated when they are, in fact, complex. They assume the solution to every problem is loads of pizza, planning, and a Gannt chart. In fact, many of today's business problems are best served by just getting started as quickly as possible, experimenting, and adjusting direction as teams learn from doing.

The more complex (unpredictable) the work is, the more it will benefit from experimentation. But this often flies directly in the face of what finance and senior executives are demanding of the teams below them. They want certainty. But because certainty is impossible, the more they push for it, the more they get fiction in return. The exercise of creating that fiction wastes valuable time and creates disengagement, cynicism, and unnecessary stress. And for what? A date that has about a 90 percent chance of being way off? A missed commitment that dispirits the team?

Great leaders at all levels of the organization know the difference between complex and complicated work. They adjust their expectations of teams accordingly. They educate and protect the teams from anyone asking for fictional commitments.

Growth vs. Fixed Mindset

In her groundbreaking book *Mindset*, Dr. Carol Dweck outlines the two basic mindsets that people tend to have as they navigate learning, trying, failing, and other aspects of life. In the *growth mindset*, one sees skill as a learned behavior. In the *fixed mindset*, people believe skills are born talents—you either have them or you don't—and that some people are naturally gifted, while others are not.

We all exist somewhere on the spectrum between these two mindsets and can shift between them depending on the day, the topic, or many other circumstances. But Dweck's research reveals that we all tend to generally gravitate towards a default stance, which is often greatly influenced by our upbringing.

If, as children, we believed our parents withheld love and affection from us for poor *results*, regardless of the *effort* we put in, or told us we were smart without understanding the importance of effort, we will likely have a fixed mindset as adults. If our parents showed us love and affection when we failed—as long as we put in the effort—we learned that trying is the important thing, and we're more likely to have a growth mindset as adults.

Those with a fixed mindset often take the safer path, resist change, and avoid doing things they may not succeed at. Those with a growth mindset are less likely to shy away from something merely because they may not succeed at it. When they are standing at the edge of their skills or knowledge, they are not scared by this fact but energized by it. They know that failure is a part of learning and that enough of it will build skills and make them better. Dweck's research found that children with a growth mindset were likely to be more successful later in life than those with a fixed mindset.

Some years ago, I taught this material to a team. There was one person on the team whom I'd spotted as a fixed mindset early on. He was very protective of the status quo and pushed back strongly on any changes that were proposed. He was good at his job, but he didn't want to learn anything new or try another approach to his work. The week after the class, he approached me and said, "I read Carol Dweck's book over the weekend, and I have a feeling this is going to change my life."

"How so?" I asked.

"As I thought through my past," he said, "I realized that I've always taken the safest path for my ego. I applied to colleges I knew would accept me and chose a major that didn't challenge me. After college, I took the jobs I knew I could perform well in. All because I was afraid of failing. I'm realizing that I'm behaving that way on this team. I'm the one pushing back on anything new because I'm afraid. I'm aware of it now and am working on changing my attitude."

This was truly a life-changing new awareness for him personally and it deeply benefitted his team.

Good leaders understand that company cultures can have growth or fixed mindsets too. Show me a culture where outcomes are rewarded (usually with bonuses and promotions) and effort isn't, and I'll show you a fixed mindset culture that discourages risk, suffers from poor innovation, encourages political games, and motivates employees to behave with a fixed mindset—even if they otherwise have growth mindsets. Bad incentives often make good people act badly.

Leaders' own mindsets are the largest contributing factor to the cultures in their organizations. If you're a leader with a fixed mindset, you will incentivize all the wrong behaviors and promote all the wrong people. Do this long enough and from a high enough position on the org chart and the entire culture will shift to a fixed mindset at your company.

A growth mindset can be learned (or a fixed one unlearned if you prefer). Good leaders spot fixed mindsets in themselves and their employees and work hard to make it safe to fail. Only then will employees begin trying innovative things. You won't beat your competition if your employees are only doing what's predictable and safe.

DEEPER DIVE

Mindset: The New Psychology of Success by Carol Dweck

Trust and Organizational Health

Over the years, I've developed a keen sense of which organizations are capable of high performance and which are not. The single most reliable predictor of high performance is the presence of trust. Patrick Lencioni describes the connection between trust and performance in his book *The Five Dysfunctions of a Team*. Put simply, if I don't trust you, I will avoid conflict with you and refrain from speaking my mind. Because I won't speak up, you'll assume my silence means agreement when it doesn't. I'll then withhold my commitment and, when things go badly, I'll avoid team accountability and focus on my own. Lencioni says that some of the most dysfunctional teams he's ever seen *never argue*. Think about that.

For clarity, Lencioni isn't talking about predictability trust. That's the trust we have that we can predict the behavior of another person. He's not talking about credibility trust, where we trust that our coworkers know what they're doing. The kind of trust he's talking about here is vulnerability trust. That kind of trust is evident when a team member can safely say, "I screwed up" or "I don't know how to do that" or "I need help." When people feel safe to be vulnerable with one another, they can let down their guard and use that energy to instead focus on the work at hand.

There is empirical evidence that if this kind of trust is not present, your teams have no chance of becoming high performing. In 2015, Google released an internal study where they conducted over 200 interviews with more than 180 Google teams. They were in search of a reproduceable way to make high performing teams. They hypothesized that the makeup of the skills on the team would be the primary ingredient. They were wrong. Instead, they found that who is on a team matters less than how the team members interact, structure their work, and view their contributions. They learned that there are five characteristics of all high performing teams:[36]

1. **Psychological Safety (Lencioni's vulnerability trust):** *Can we take risks on this team without feeling insecure or embarrassed?*

2. **Dependability:** *Can we count on each other to do high quality work on time?*

3. **Structure and Clarity:** *Are goals, roles, and execution plans on our team clear?*

4. **Meaning of work:** *Are we working on something that is personally important for each of us?*

5. **Impact of work:** *Do we fundamentally believe that the work we're doing matters to the team?*

Number one on the list is trust. Put simply, people who trust one another can move mountains. People who do not trust one another will make mountains out of molehills. As a leader, you are in a powerful position to either create an environment where trust like this will grow or one where it won't even get a chance to bud. Good leaders know that trust is like oxygen for a team. If it's present, no one will think about it. If it's missing, it's all that anyone will think about. These leaders know that true connection between employees takes time and organizational stability. And it usually happens much faster in person. Which leads me to . . .

A Note About Remote Teams

The COVID pandemic has deeply affected many of us. Many team members have been working from home for much of the time. I want to take a moment to address a few popular and perhaps unpopular realities associated with this development.

---

[36] Natasha Tamiru, "Team Dynamics: Five Keys to Building Effective Teams," *Think with Google* (blog), entry posted June 2023, accessed March 7, 2024, https://www.thinkwithgoogle.com/intl/en-emea/consumer-insights/consumer-trends/five-dynamics-effective-team/.

From most employees' perspectives—especially introverts—working from home is almost all benefits and no downsides. Drastic positive financial impacts have been realized by workers who have reduced their childcare costs, eliminated commutes, or moved to other areas or even other states with lower costs of living. In some cases, this makes for less stress too. It's tempting to think we should continue like this forever. Even employers can benefit financially with reduced capital expenses. What could go wrong?

For starters, it's important to realize that many of the teams who were working remotely at the first part of the pandemic started out working together in an office first prior to COVID. Whatever trust they had built for each other in person endured any time and distance. It's entirely different to form a team whose members have never met in person and expect that same level of trust and performance from them.

As we have continued to work remotely, more and more of our teams consist of people who have never met in person. You may be saying, "So?" Here's where I must break the bad news. We're social creatures. We've developed key psychological behaviors—even trust itself—as a way of deeply connecting with "us" in our tribe while being wary of "them" in their tribe. We have evolved a lightning-fast, subconscious perception of many nonverbal cues from others that our limbic brain processes as a feeling before our prefrontal cortex can get the news. When we "trust our instincts" about another person, we're really inventorying a lot of subtle data we've detected about that person and pattern-matching it to our past experiences with others.

When we were all in the office, it wasn't the work we did under the same roof that built our vulnerability trust for one another, it was the sitting together and asking, "So what did you do over the weekend?" and then discovering that our coworker also likes axe throwing and that we play the same video games. That may have prompted a weekend hangout where our partners met each other and friendships were built. Or perhaps we were there to witness their processing of a death in the family, a divorce, or another big life challenge.

From these kinds of moments, coworkers learn that it's safe to be vulnerable with one another, and the resulting connection can move mountains. Remote work is making it very difficult to establish that connection.

Companies do successfully pull off full-time remote work—Automattic, the makers of WordPress come to mind as they have over a thousand employees spread across seventy-plus countries—but these companies spend a lot of time, money, and effort creating in-person connections that being in an office together can create on its own.[37]

Before you toss this book into a burning fire, I'm not arguing that all of us should come into the office again. The benefits to employees of having flexibility to work remotely are undeniable and the practice should be continued. I suspect that most companies and employees will discover that a hybrid model works best in which some or all employees work from outside the office but also come together regularly. Just one week per quarter with the whole team together at the same time would make a huge difference.

What companies will continue to find challenging is the situation where some employees are in the office, and some are permanently remote. In this scenario, the people in the room together are communicating verbally and nonverbally at a depth that far exceeds what's happening across a video call. In a room, we can understand multiple people talking over one another. Over a video conference, it sounds like gibberish. The remote people also can't easily read faces; they have a view of a table at the home office with tiny faces, all contained in a window on their screen. That window is made even smaller when someone starts sharing their screen. Sprinkle in unstable Internet or other

---

[37] For an interesting talk on the subject, listen to Sam Harris interview Automattic CEO Matt Mullenweg on his podcast:
https://podcasts.apple.com/us/podcast/distributed-with-matt-mullenweg/id1463243282?i=1000471601774

technical challenges and it's a recipe for shallow, broken-tempo conversations.

You might be asking, how is that different from the overseas teams we were working with before COVID? It isn't. But then I'd ask how that was working out for everyone. It's outside the scope of this book to go into great depth about the questionable wisdom of globalizing, outsourcing, and physically dividing our teams. Peter Cappelli does a nice job of that in the Deeper Dive below. I'll just say that the costs of time zone synchronization; language barriers; poor internet connectivity; lack of trust and connection; increased handoffs; cultural differences in business practices; lack of ownership from contractors; and big disconnects between product and delivery all add up to a huge undocumented loss of productivity, quality, and speed in most instances. That isn't an argument not to have overseas teams, but it is an argument to have those teams be either completely there or completely here. Making a team a combination of onshore and offshore makes the downsides I just described a near certainty.

Here's what I know for certain: We will not overcome over two million years of evolved social instinct because a pandemic forced us to use video conferencing effectively for a couple years. We must either acknowledge that high-performing teams require vulnerability trust that is most effectively built by spending regular time together in person—again, even one week per quarter would suffice—or redefine our definition of high-performing teams. Companies like Automattic solved many of the challenges to remote work even before the pandemic. But I believe their CEO, Matt Mullenweg, would be the first to say that it requires money and effort to be a company that can work 100 percent remotely while still building connection. Oh, and for the record, Automattic still brings employees physically together regularly.

I did a miniseries about remote work on my YouTube channel. Check it out, along with some other helpful resources, in this deeper dive:

> **DEEPER DIVE**
>
> *Our Least Important Asset: Why the Relentless Focus on Finance and Accounting Is Bad for Business and Employees* by Peter Cappelli
>
> *The Five Dysfunctions of a Team* by Patrick Lencioni
>
> *The Power of Vulnerability (Audiobook)* by Brené Brown
>
> *YouTube mini-series on remote work:*
> https://www.youtube.com/@MotivatedOutcomes

Less Is More

When I graduated from high school, I became a certified sound engineer. This meant that, among other things, I learned to operate those giant mixing consoles you see in music studios and at concert events. When I got my training in live concert engineering (called sound reinforcement), my mentor explained that during concerts, it's important to remember that *less is more*. He explained that some sound engineers get that backwards. An engineer will be listening to the concert and notice that he or she can't hear the guitar very well, so they'll nudge up the level. Then they notice that the vocals are too low and nudge those up too. Then the keyboard player. Each volume movement is solving the immediate issue, but the overall level of the concert is slowly rising to eardrum-bleeding levels in a race to eleven[38]. Instead, what the good sound engineer asks is *why can't I hear the guitar?* Could it be because another instrument is too loud? Perhaps if I pull another instrument *down*, balance will be restored. In music mixing, less is often more.

Leaders can fall into the same trap. They create (or allow to be created) systems and/or team formations that require immense coordination, which means hiring more program managers and creating an entire organization of managers,

---

[38] Pardon the *This is Spinal Tap* reference.

directors, senior directors, vice presidents, and senior vice presidents. All those new hires require more human resources people and buildings to house them all, which means more janitorial staff and so on.

I understand the trap. Leaders think they're doing the right thing. Their employees are asking for help. The need could be very real and, like nudging the guitar volume up a bit, additional staff could provide immediate relief. Good leaders know to *always watch the system*. They ask, "What is it about our system that is making you need more people?" and "Is there something we could *remove* that would increase the flow of work without adding headcount?" When it comes to the systemic challenges that leaders are responsible for fixing, many times less is more.

Leadership Stances

The last concept good leaders know well is that they can lead from several "positions" or stances, each with their own benefits and drawbacks. Figuratively speaking, leaders can lead from the front, the side, the back, or the top. Let's discuss each in turn.

Leading From the Front

Leaders who lead from the front have a "follow me" vibe. They don't command followers; they lead by example. They are leaders *because people are behind them* not because they stepped in front of others. This stance is what's called for when organizations are in disarray or when they aren't clear about their vision—what Simon Sinek would call the company's just cause. Leading from the front means teaching, mentoring, and guiding. Leaders with compelling visions begin by leading from the front. The plan is not to stay there, however. Leaders who stay in the front create a shadow that new leaders cannot emerge from. The goal of the front leadership stance is to inspire employees and ignite the leader in each of *them*.

Leading From the Side

Leaders who lead from the side have a "let's do this together" vibe. They see new leaders emerging to carry the vision forward and want to lead *with* them. Being at their side lends them credibility with the rest of the employees and supports them while they become proficient. The plan is not to stay there either. Leaders who stay on the side too long are like a set of training wheels that need to come off. The goal of the side leadership stance is to support and promote others.

Leading From the Back

Leaders who lead from the back have an "I have your back, but you've got this" vibe. They know their employees are aligned with their vision and are ready to run with it. Leaders who lead from the back are closest to servant leadership, but I prefer Mark McKergow's term "host leadership." Hosts are still in charge, but their sole responsibility is bringing people together and creating a productive working environment for their employees. We'll discuss this in more detail in Chapter 12, but host leaders are there to ensure that everyone has what they need and will step in for support at any time, but they are intentionally in the background allowing others to operate autonomously. This stance empowers and trusts others. If there was a stance to rest on, this would be it.

Leading From the Top

Leading from the top has a "no time for questions, do as I tell you" vibe. While this hero leadership stance is useful for very specific conditions (e.g., the Cynefin chaos quadrant), its useful life is very short. Besides, if your company is truly in chaos all the time, you've got bigger problems. It takes almost no time for employees to begin resenting a top-down leader. Spend too much time in this stance and your employees will begin to feel like a disempowered, micromanaged set of hands rather than a group of brains. Top-down leadership is appropriate for team health problems, disruptive employees, and human resources/performance issues. If it were only used in these instances, the working world would be a better place. Unfortunately, it is the most overused leadership stance. Too many leaders use this stance because they either like controlling other people or they feel accountable for results and don't trust their teams to get the work done.

Stance Switching: The Leadership Two-Step

Great leaders are proficient at holding any of these stances and can move between them as needed. Like a parent teaching their child to ride a bike, they know how to inspire, run alongside, then remove the training wheels and stand back. They only step in again if things get wobbly. These stances are powerful reminders that true leadership responds to what the organization needs, not what fulfills the leader's ego. Performing a dance called the Leadership Two-Step, these leaders step forward when they need to and then step back to guide and support. Leaders who cannot switch stances are like hammers that make every situation and every person into a nail.

Summarizing the Basics

If you got through this chapter about these aspects of work and how they form organizational values and mindsets and you learned some things, congratulations and please don't judge yourself. Leaders who understand and have strong values about every one of these aspects are rare. In fact, I believe we're suffering from a leadership crisis in the world because of how rare it is to deeply understand each of these concepts—and we still have more to cover, these were just the basics. Let's recap:

Great Leaders:

- **Understand the difference between efficiency and effectiveness.** They want efficiency, but they want effectiveness more.
- **Know the difference between outputs and outcomes.** They keep their eye on the goal, not on the steps to get

there.
- **Know the difference between complicated and complex work** and understand how each type affects their own expectations from teams.
- **Have a growth mindset and understand how a fixed one gets in the way of growth**—for their companies, for themselves, and for their employees.
- **Understand trust and its relation to team performance**. They encourage and practice vulnerability that fosters trust and fuels continuous improvement.
- **Know that less is often more.** They understand that adding is easy. Subtracting to add is harder, but often more valuable.
- **Understand the four leadership stances** and when to use each one. They see themselves as hosts rather than dictators or servants.

Chapter 12: Successful Leadership Behaviors

It doesn't make sense to hire smart people and tell them what to do. We hire smart people so they can tell us what to do.

– Steve Jobs

When asked to rate their own driving skills, most drivers report that they are above average. Setting aside the fact that it's statistically impossible for most drivers to be above average in the first place, why do some drivers think they are better than they are? When rated on a standard scale, most drivers who scored low would likely criticize the scale rather than their own driving—their egos stepping in to save the day.

Similarly, when I poll leaders to ask if they believe they are good servant leaders, most raise their hands. Yet here we are suffering from a dearth of good leadership and have employee turnover levels we haven't seen in decades—if ever. It seems we've taught everyone a good buzzword, but training and accountability are missing.

Perhaps part of the problem is with the term itself. *Servant* has a negative connotation or "less than" vibe for many people. Asking leaders, many of whom are already struggling with their need to feel important, to assume a position they view as "less than" with their employees is destined to be met with resistance, at minimum subconsciously. On top of that, there *is a place and time* for leaders to step up to the front of the room and lead, but servants don't do that, do they?

As I mentioned in the previous chapter, Mark McKergow agrees that the term "servant leader" isn't doing the job and prefers host leader. As a host, we want our party guests to be comfortable, but we don't want to control their behavior moment by moment. We bring them together, and we may step forward to the front of the room, but then we step back to allow the guests to mingle and define their experience. As I mentioned earlier, when leaders do this dance, I call it the leadership two-step.

If leaders ran their dinner parties the way most of them run their organizations, I doubt that they'd have many guests wanting to show up at future parties. McKergow is right. Host is a better term, and it more aptly describes what leaders need to be doing. In Chapter 11, we covered some important concepts that too many well-intentioned leaders ignore, have backwards, or simply don't understand. In this chapter, we're going to talk about behaviors of great leaders.

One quick note before we move into the material. If you read anything in this chapter and disagree with the recommended behavior, I'd challenge you to consider what underlying values and beliefs you have that make the behavior feel wrong to you. It's completely possible that the behavior won't work for you. It's also possible we're pushing against a belief you haven't challenged recently—if ever.

> **DEEPER DIVE**
>
> *Host Leadership: Six New Roles of Engagement for Teams, Organizations, Communities, and Movements* by Mark McKergow

The Gardner vs. The Chess Player

My peers and clients often call me "The Analogy King" as analogies seem to pop into my head quite often to explain complex topics in very relatable, memorable, and sometimes funny ways. So, I was deeply drawn into General Stanley McChrystal's gardener analogy from his book *Team of Teams: New Rules of Engagement for a Complex World.* I've already compared being a leader to being a gardener in this book and this is the origin of it. McChrystal writes:

> The temptation to lead as a chess master, controlling each move of the organization, must give way to an approach as a gardener, enabling rather than directing. A gardening approach to leadership is anything but passive. The leader acts as an "eyes-on, hands-off" enabler who creates and maintains an ecosystem in which the organization operates. [...] The gardener cannot actually grow tomatoes, squash, or beans. She can only foster an environment in which the plants do so.[39]

---

[39] Stanley A. McChrystal, *Team of Teams: The Power of Small Groups in a Fragmented World* (London: Portfolio, 2015), [Page 220].

McChrystal spends an entire chapter explaining the idea and how it transformed his leadership, but what it took to light me up was just that one paragraph. If many of today's leaders were gardeners, they'd surely try screaming at the tomatoes to make them grow. I confess that the image of that makes me laugh every time I imagine it. "Grow, damnit!" I wish that yelling at the tomatoes was the worst mistake these leaders made. Too many are *poisoning the soil* these plants are in and then wondering why they won't grow, then blaming the plants. They've completely misunderstood their role in the process. I'll repeat Simon Sinek's quote here again because it's relevant: "Leaders are not responsible for the results. Leaders are responsible for the *people* who are responsible for the results."

I mention the gardener analogy here because, as you read the behaviors in this chapter, you'll need to shift your entire idea of what successful leaders *do* in complex environments. When you accept this analogy, it may become more apparent to you when you are figuratively yelling at tomatoes or even poisoning the soil, all the while ignoring the important duties of cultivating and protecting the environment where the work occurs.

The Four Basic Leadership Behaviors

As I've mentioned several times, human beings are complex. Throw in complex organizations operating in complex markets and you've really got to marvel at how it all comes together every day. In the face of all this complexity, it would be an oversimplification for me to simply list off a bunch of behaviors and assure you that they will work. There are, however, four basic behaviors that leaders can adopt that will drastically improve their leadership and, by extension, the experience of those they lead:

1. Create effective organizations
2. Lead ethically
3. Connect people with meaning
4. Coach, don't play

Create Effective Organizations

In Chapter 11, we discussed the idea of effectiveness versus efficiency. The concept is so important and so overlooked that I'm going to repeat it here. Efficiency is about utilization. Effectiveness is about value. So many leaders are operating with the idea that efficiency *is the value* that I sometimes wonder if business schools are stuck in the industrial revolution era. Most companies don't make money by keeping everyone busy. They make money by delivering a product or a service. In fact, often the busier the employees are, the slower the product or service is delivered. Packing a freeway to 100 percent capacity is an *efficient* use of the pavement and a very *ineffective* way to move cars. I believe effective organizations have the following:

- **Competent missionaries**: Effective organizations hire, train, and retain missionaries not mercenaries.
- **Empowerment**: Competent employees collaborate with leaders to determine how they organize to deliver value.
- **A systems view**: They are continuously refining and optimizing the system, not just the teams inside of it.
- **A vigilant watch for poison**: Everyone is on the lookout for people who detract from team synergy.

Competent Missionaries

What do we mean when we say competent? I define competent as the ability to effectively and efficiently get a job done autonomously. Importantly, in a complex business environment, here's what it *doesn't* mean:

- Agreeing with the leader.
- Doing what the leader would have done.
- Following instructions.
- Being fast (speed is one outcome of competence but speed alone is not competence).
- Remaining quiet in the face of disagreement.
- Focusing on outputs over outcomes.

It's important not to mistake a lack of enthusiasm or engagement for incompetence. Competent employees will be severely demotivated by a lack of empowerment. Conversely, don't mistake credentials (names of previous employers or universities where degrees were earned) for competence. Some of the worst leaders and disruptive team members I've seen have top-notch pedigrees. I'm not saying that there aren't great leaders and competent employees from Ivy League schools. I'm saying that coming from an Ivy League school doesn't itself make you a great leader or a competent employee.

As for the second word, missionaries, we are looking for people who understand and believe in our company's just cause. Not just people who check the boxes for skills we need. I hate to break some bad news here but physical distance matters. Outsourcing important parts of your product or service creation to faraway countries to save money means that you're often hiring mercenaries offshore and saddling your missionaries onshore with all the ensuing time zone and language barrier problems. The cost savings show up on the profit and loss statement, but the lost productivity and innovation do not.

Empowerment

There is no better illustration of empowerment done right than David Marquet's book *Turn the Ship Around*. In it, Captain Marquet was put into the unenviable position of being placed in charge of a $2.8 billion nuclear class submarine that he did not fully understand. He had been preparing for taking command of a different sub and could have told you where every wire went and what every button and knob did. But the last-minute switch to a different sub left him feeling unprepared. He knew it and his crew knew it.

Captain Marquet and his leadership team reasoned that they needed a new way of running the sub that departed from tradition. So, they created a rather unorthodox method called intent-based leadership. In this style, crew members would call out their intent and the captain would acknowledge. This is the opposite of how things normally operate on a sub—and yet it worked. In his widely viewed YouTube talk called *Greatness*, Marquet says:[40]

> On another submarine, there was one guy in charge. One guy giving orders. One guy thinking, and 134 people doing what they're told. I don't care how smart you are. On my submarine, I've got 135 thinking, active, passionate, creative, proactive, taking initiative people. It's a tidal wave! You don't stand a chance.

Marquet says that we're genetically and culturally programmed to "take control and attract followers" when what we really need to do is "give control and create leaders." And it seems like he might know what he's talking about: under intent-based leadership, his submarine went from one of the worst in the Navy to the highest-rated submarine in Navy history.

In his book *Everybody Matters*, Bob Chapman describes empowerment this way:[41]

> There are two kinds of freedom: "freedom from" and "freedom to." Freedom from is about freeing people from excessive hierarchy, burdensome rules, stifling bureaucracy, and depression. A command-and-control management style imposes many such curbs on freedom in the workplace. We should remove as many of these constraints as possible from every work environment.
>
> While "freedom from" liberates individuals from oppressive rules, it does not by itself provide opportunities for them to express themselves. This is where a "freedom to" comes in. People should have the freedom to innovate, experiment, and fail. But in the absence of shared values and a moral compass, "freedom to" can degenerate into self-serving anarchy. Dov Siedman says, "a handful of shared values is worth more than 1,000 rules."

A Systems View

I'm not a pilot but I play one on my computer. I'm a flight simulator enthusiast and have even built my own cockpit at

---

[40] "MindSpring Presents: 'Greatness' by David Marquet," video, 09:47, *YouTube*, posted by MindSpring, October 8, 2013, accessed June 16, 2022, https://www.youtube.com/watch?v=OqmdLcyES_Q.

[41] Chapman and Sisodia, *Everybody Matters*, [Page 176].

home. I fly planes of all sizes including my favorite, the Airbus A320. Because this is a hobby of mine, I also follow aviation influencers—often real airline pilots—on YouTube. These pilots tend to make videos about airline crashes or mishaps, reconstructing them with expertise that's unmatched by any news reports of these events. It sounds morbid but I assure you that the best way to become good at anything is to deeply study failures—our own and those of others. One of the reasons that commercial air travel is so safe is that after every accident or near accident, the incident is thoroughly investigated by aviation experts including air traffic control, aeronautical engineers, and pilots. These investigations have a lot of data to work with. All radio traffic and cockpit dialog are recorded, and the flight data recorder on commercial planes are recording a minimum of eighty-eight data points and some are recording over a thousand more.

After watching many of these videos over the years, I've come to understand how this mountain of data is used to determine root causes of the incident. Rarely are accidents the cause of a single problem. They are usually a cascade of errors that all happen in sequence, sometimes with different human beings each making a single error. Airline crash investigations conducted by the National Transportation and Safety Board (NTSB) are always centered on at least three main categories: people, equipment, and the system these people and equipment are operating in. It is not unheard of for a single crash to result in changes to equipment, pilot training, air traffic control procedure, and/or airport equipment. While pilot error is involved in roughly 88 percent of chartered plane crashes, it is often a contributing factor rather than the sole reason.

You might be thinking, *This is fascinating Sean but what does it have to do with leadership?* I want to reiterate a point I just made using different words: The reason air accidents result in a safer industry is because investigators use their data to study the people *and* the system.

How does this differ from how leaders in business handle failures? Today's leaders often focus very much on the people when things are going wrong without taking the time to look at the system the people are operating inside of. That would be like the NTSB focusing solely on the pilots after each crash. Ignoring the system is likely ignoring a giant lever that greatly impacts many people. It is the system that impacts the efficiency and effectiveness of the people operating inside of it, and yet these systems often just evolve into existence rather than being thoughtfully designed. Their influence on the people operating inside of them are often an afterthought.

Repeatedly, I see leaders set up their organizations by grouping similar skills into teams, then having the work pass from team to team. The analogy of making a cup of coffee is useful here. We can either set up a hot water team, a coffee bean team, a sugar team, and a cream team and then pass the cup from team to team, or we can assemble teams each made up of a hot water person, a coffee bean person, a sugar person, and a cream person and let them pass the cup between each specialist. In which scenario will we have a cup of coffee faster? It's true that each person on that mixed skills team will be idle while waiting for the cup and after passing it on, but is the value keeping everyone busy (efficiency) or is it a fast, hot cup of coffee (effectiveness)?

The cost in time and effort that a system imposes upon employees and customers is not invisible. I'm sure you can relate to calling a company's customer service number only to be transferred from one team to another as each team specializes in certain aspects of the problem you're experiencing. That's quite efficient for the company but very ineffective for you the customer. Their system design is causing those transfers.

Because it's a simpler problem to address a team or a team member than it is to address the systems these employees operate inside of, many leaders willfully ignore the systemic problems to focus on the parts inside. Frequently, that's in no small part because these leaders played a part in creating the system that isn't working well. They created the organizational structure that looked great on a spreadsheet but is slowing the work to a crawl. They hired the leaders inside the organization who are poisoning it. Facing their own accountability for the system's design is much more difficult than blaming the parts inside it.

You can put the most talented people into teams with the best equipment, but if you drop those teams into a terrible system, the work will come out slower and with poorer quality. Effective organizations ensure that the system is always being looked at for improvements. As Dr. W Edwards Deming, a noted management consultant, said in 1993, "A bad system will beat a good person every time."

A Vigilant Watch for Poison

We touched upon keeping an eye out for poisonous people earlier when we discussed brilliant assholes. I'm repeating it here because it's a reminder that sometimes the most additive thing you can do to increase team synergy is subtract someone who's getting in the way. More to the point of this book, *this is even more important when the person in question holds a leadership position, because they are a drop of poison in your organization.*

The insidious way that poisonous leaders get into companies means that every leader—if not every employee—must be on the lookout for it. Every policy and incentive plan must be examined for how it could potentially incentivize poisonous behaviors. If your company values outcomes at all costs, then it will incentivize leaders to churn through burnt-out employees for increased profit. It will attract and promote results-driven people into leadership roles.

It's not that being results-driven is bad, but 99 percent of the time the results being driven towards don't include employee happiness and engagement. If they did, I'd be all for a results-driven leader.

The Illusion of Understanding Strikes Again

While creating effective organizations is a leadership responsibility, I don't want to suggest that you should become a Chess Master leader, disappear into a cave, draw pretty org charts on the wall, then roll out a new organization. This is a common mistake I see leaders make. They think it's their job to put the plan together and the employees' jobs to fall in line. Instead, it is a leader's job to repeatedly remind everyone why they're there, stress the effectiveness over efficiency goal of the organization, then trust their employees to have them participate in how they're organized to succeed. Leaders can offer a framework, guidelines, guardrails, or whatever other euphemism you wish to use, but they cannot understand every facet of the work the way employees who do the work can. The higher you get in rank, the more you need to trust your frontline employees to help you realize the goals you're setting.

Lead Ethically

One of the ways that systems can be dysfunctional is through ethical fading. According to the University of Texas:

> Ethical fading occurs when the ethical aspects of a decision disappear from view. This happens when people focus heavily on some other aspect of a decision, such as profitability or winning. People tend to see what they are looking for, and if they are not looking for an ethical issue, they may miss it altogether.[42]

We likely don't need to spend too much time defining this behavior as it is the plot line of most movies and TV shows. Most villains and even some protagonists have a moral flaw they struggle with . . . some means that they justify with some end. Even the infamous Thanos finger snap that removed half the people from the universe made sense to him (if you're not a Marvel fan, just ignore me). We can spot the failing when it happens in others, but we often fail to see it when it's our own behavior that's unethical. We are *very* good at explaining away our own ethical failing in fact—and that's the problem.

---

[42] McCombs School of Business, "Ethical Fading," Ethics Unwrapped, last modified 2023, accessed August 29, 2023, https://ethicsunwrapped.utexas.edu/glossary/ethical-fading.

While I've known about the behavior for some time, I first learned the term "ethical fading" from Simon Sinek in his excellent book *The Infinite Game*. In it, he dives deeply into a great example of corporate ethical fading in the 2016 Wells Fargo scandal that eventually resulted in over fifty-three hundred employees being fired and $185 million in fines. As it turns out, the unethical behavior involved was known about and tacitly approved of—if not encouraged—all the way up to then CEO John Stumpf.

The unethical behavior of opening millions of accounts for customers without their knowledge or approval resulted in a blinding amount of money for most involved. People involved in the scandal ranged from unwilling participants pressured to do so with the threat of losing their jobs to the most senior executives who turned a blind eye to the behavior in return for massive profits and the bonuses tied to them. It's called ethical *fading* because it's not usually something that turns on or off like a switch. One unpunished sellout to ethics at the right level causes a trickle down of shoulder-shrugging and excuse-making and before you know it, the entire company is now behaving unethically.

Ethical fading is usually a one-two punch of an incentive or reward combined with a person who sees no way to achieve the outcome without a little cheating. Euphemisms and victim stories are very helpful to convince the person that the cheating is justified and not hurting anyone. If there are victims, they are reduced to account numbers or completely dehumanized to remove any chance of second thoughts about the behavior.

If it's not obvious to you yet, let me be clear: Ethical fading is a form of poison in an organization.

Lest you believe that you would never behave this way, a controversial experiment in the 1960s known as the Milgram experiment, named after the Yale professor who conducted the study, Dr. Stanley Milgram, showed that 65 percent of participants in the study would deliver maximum electrical shocks to other human beings under the right circumstances. None of the participants were sadists. They were simply visually shielded from viewing the pain they were inflicting and were influenced by an authority figure who told them that what they were doing was ok. More recent studies have concluded that the degree to which we obey the questionable orders of an authority figure depends upon the degree to which we agree with the order and how much we identify with the person giving the orders.

Interestingly, later experiments by Milgram showed that the presence of rebellious peers dramatically reduced obedience levels. When other people refused to go along with the experimenters' orders, thirty-six out of forty participants refused to deliver the maximum shocks.[43] This really sends home the point that ethical fading can be prevented or curtailed by a strong ethical culture. We do it once and no one says anything, so we may do it again. But if someone does say something, we are less likely to do so.

High turnover and reduced innovation are not the only ways that a poisonous leader can kill your company. Unethical behavior can become pervasive through their example, causing otherwise ethical people to mirror the unethical behavior because "everyone does it here." Be on the lookout for the first hints of unethical behavior and make examples of those who introduce it to your organization.

DEEPER DIVE

The Infinite Game by Simon Sinek

Connect People with Meaning

Early in my career in the mid 1990s, I was a desktop support engineer. Basically, the guy you called when your computer wasn't working or needed to be installed. I handled everything from the servers to the network closet to the desktop computer or

---

[43] Kendra Cherry, MSEd, "What Was the Milgram Experiment?" Verywell Mind, last modified November 14, 2022, accessed August 29, 2023, https://www.verywellmind.com/the-milgram-obedience-experiment-2795243.

laptop at the end of the line. I happened to be doing this kind of work when the company I was working for, a major Silicon Valley company, was relocating its headquarters to a brand-new facility in downtown San Jose, CA. It was a huge undertaking requiring an immense amount of coordination between movers, electricians, network engineers, and folks like me. Several thousand people would be relocated over the course of just a single week.

What became evident very quickly was that the way our group was coordinating the move was not working. It was basically an Excel spreadsheet and lots and lots of radio calls to a person updating that sheet and dispatching people.

At the time, I had dabbled in using an application called FileMaker Pro—a rapid development database system. I had used it to make all kinds of databases at home for tracking comic books, movie collections, home inventory, recipes, etc. I really had a passion for keeping information organized and searchable. I spotted the disorganization and knew I could design something to help. I mentioned it to my boss at the time and he asked, "How fast can you build something for me to look at?" I said I could have a basic system the following day. I was not quite sure if he believed me, but I was pleased that he gave me the go-ahead to proceed.

I was up most of the night, and the next day I came in with a database that the teams could use to track the readiness of the various offices and cubicles. Rather than having to make a radio call to get the status of an office, each group could check the database to search for offices ready for them. The process worked amazingly well. I continued to hone and improve it that next day. In the end, we estimated that we saved an entire day's labor for our team of fifty engineers and movers by having this system in place. The experience led me to ultimately change my career to becoming a full-time database engineer for nearly a decade.

How did my boss at the time get such amazing results from me? By allowing me to follow my passion. He could have just as easily seen it as too big of a risk to lose one of his engineers during a crucial project with a tight deadline, but he could read the passion and confidence in my face. That, among other things, is what made him a great leader. It paid off for him and for me.

There will be no faster and more intrinsic way for you to get your employees to be high performing and engaged than for you to connect their work to something meaningful to them. If you're the leader of a brand-new startup, you're likely already attracting people who have connected your just cause to their personal meaning and are putting in long hours as a result. Startups usually have a lot of "founder's fire" that is quite contagious to employees. But after a company has been around for a while, a growing disconnection can occur as the founder moves on and that fire gets harder to find. It follows, then, that most leaders probably have employees who collect a check and do good work but who aren't sure how their work connects in any meaningful way to the personal impact these employees want to make in the world.

I don't want to make it sound like there's anything wrong with collecting a check and "just" doing your job. If you're not feeling a yearning or dissatisfaction from that, then, carry on. But studies suggest that 85 percent of global workers are dissatisfied with their jobs. I believe this is mostly a failure of leadership rather than a failure of these employees. To be sure, there are people who haven't done the inner work to really understand what makes them tick. The entire life coaching industry deals with this one issue most of the time. Once coaches connect people to their values and meaning, they're usually off to the races, quitting their jobs, finding meaningful work, and taking themselves out of that 85 percent.

I think this reality creates an opportunity for leaders. When I lead teams, I take care to understand those who report to me. What makes them tick? What do they enjoy doing when they're not working and why do they do those things? I'm not learning these things to manipulate them but to see if there's a way to connect what they do for me to something they already enjoy. Am I unaware of a passion they have? Is there a way I could alter the job they do for me that would harness that passion? The best leaders I've had across my entire career have been the ones who saw a fire in me and learned to harness it for the company's goals. When that happened, I never felt manipulated. Quite the opposite. I felt rejuvenated, validated, and rewarded.

Be that kind of leader for people who work for you. Take a chance on their ideas. Make it safe for them to fail while encouraging them to try. See something in them that they may not yet see in themselves.

Coach, Don't Play

I come from a long line of soccer players. In fact, my grandfather was a player for the famous Feyenoord Rotterdam soccer team in Holland prior to WWII. My parents both played. So, me joining a team when I was five was a foregone conclusion.

I'm not sure if you've ever watched a young-player soccer game but our games were usually quite comical. We had no situational awareness and barely knew the rules of the game, but there we were on the field. Our parents were on the sidelines yelling commands at us like we were remote-controlled soccer players. *Move here. Watch for the ball, it's coming your way! Run! Ok wait there. Pass to John! Now SHOOT!*

As I became a coach for business teams and their leaders, I realized that when I'm on the field, I'm not very helpful. Like our parents on the sidelines, coaches have a unique perspective of the situation on the field. They may be very vested in the outcome, but they are not the ones moving the ball. Instead, they use their perspective to help the players see how they're playing the game and working (or not working) as a team. This is an incredible responsibility and an important job.

When I was an Agile Coach, I saw many attempts by companies to collapse and eliminate the Scrum Master role or to pressure the Agile Coaches to act more like project managers (in other words, to get on the field). The logic seems simple on the surface. Why am I paying for this warm body with these skills to stand outside the game when I could put them and their knowledge *in the game?* The problem is that the very thing that was making them effective—the perspective from *outside the field*—is lost. Now they have the same blind spots that all the players have. There is a reason that all sports games usually have a camera up high in the bleachers recording the games. It's to get the perspective of the game that allows these players to see how their own view at ground level meshes with what was really going on in the game. Coaches play this role. If it isn't obvious yet, leaders are meant to be coaches, not players, so that we can capture the unique perspective that teams are missing.

I recently worked with a company that decided to collapse their engineering organization by making engineering managers into managing engineers, and oh, what a difference the word order makes. Managing engineers are expected to be hands-on-keyboard most of the time. They're super talented developers, so why not have them coding? Well, because the people who report to them are no longer getting the same level of mentorship or help with bureaucratic blocking issues, systemic problems, or any of the other important coaching duties that an engineering manager would perform. A perfect example of jumping over dollars to pick up dimes, it downplays the immense amount of skill that it takes to lead people in favor of the skills needed to write good code—something the team members should be doing under the tutelage of a good engineering manager.

Good leaders stay off the field and let the players do the playing. They use the unique perspective afforded to them by their spot on the sidelines, combined with their knowledge of the game, to help the players make better choices. There's a reason that professional sports teams pay millions of dollars for a team of coaches. They improve the performance of everyone on the field and, ultimately, the outcomes for the team.

Summary

There are four core behaviors that great leaders adopt:

- **They create effective organizations.** Effective

organizations are constructed to prioritize delivering value over keeping everyone busy. These organizations are made more effective by hiring and training competent missionaries rather than hiring mercenaries. They empower and involve employees in how they organize and deliver value. They keep a systems view and aren't afraid to examine the way a system is empowering or impeding the teams operating inside of it. Effective organizations protect their effectiveness by keeping a diligent watch for poisonous people, behavior, policies, and incentives.

- **They lead ethically.** Great leaders know that they set the tone about values in the organization. Whatever they tacitly or implicitly make okay will be adopted in the organizations they lead. They are consciously and constantly diligent about keeping their companies and teams behaving ethically.
- **They connect people with meaning.** They share and repeat their values and vision and they help to connect employees to that vision. They inspire people to solve real problems and connect them to the impact their actions are having.
- **They coach, they don't play.** They recognize that autonomy is supported when they stay off the field and is damaged when they're on it. The teams they lead recognize and appreciate their off-the-field perspective, because that perspective is only used to make them better.

DEEPER DIVE

Turn the Ship Around by David Marquet

Everybody Matters by Bob Chapman

Multipliers by Liz Wiseman

Team of Teams by General Stanley McChrystal

CHAPTER 13: A CREATOR AND DESTROYER OF WORLDS

IN THE HANDS OF MAN

He who creates a poison, also has the cure.
He who creates a virus, also has the antidote.
He who creates chaos, also has the ability to create peace.
He who sparks hate, also has the ability to transform it to love.
He who creates misery, also has the ability to destroy it with kindness.
He who creates sadness, also has the ability to convert it to happiness.
He who creates darkness, can also be awakened to produce illumination.
He who spreads fear, can also be shaken to spread comfort.
Any problems created by the left hand of man,
Can also be solved with the right,
For he who manifests anything,
Also has the ability to
Destroy it.

— Suzy Kassem[44]

---

[44] Suzy Kassem and Ryan Grim, *Rise up and Salute the Sun: The Writings of Suzy Kassem* (Boston: Awakened Press, 2011).

It is not an exaggeration to say that once people are placed in your charge, you have a large amount of power to create and destroy. However, as Uncle Ben of Spiderman lore would advise, "with great power, comes great responsibility."[45] As a leader, you are greatly responsible for creating the world people live in nearly half of their waking hours each workday. If they don't like the world you create, they will find another.

Sometimes the creations and destructions are accidental and sometimes intentional. A good leader understands the power they have, and they take it very seriously. In this chapter, we're going to go over the kind of creation and destruction power leaders have, whether they want it or not and whether they realize they have it or not. In my travels and work with others, I've concluded that the kind of world most of us want to work in is:

- Stable
- Safe
- Connected
- Clear
- Purposeful
- Impactful

It's no coincidence that Google determined many of these traits are required ingredients to have even the *possibility* of a high-performing team.[46] What is a company if not a team of teams?

Create Stability

Stability comes in two flavors, organizational stability and personal stability, and leaders play a role in the creation of both. Let's explore each in turn.

---

[45] This idea is more than comic book lore. The phrase, in different forms, dates back as far as the Christian bible. "To whomever much is given, of him will much be required; and to whom much was entrusted, of him more will be asked." (Luke 12:48).

[46] See https://www.thinkwithgoogle.com/intl/en-emea/consumer-insights/consumer-trends/five-dynamics-effective-team/

Organizational Stability

I once worked with a company that, I was convinced, believed that its mission wasn't to deliver product to a market, it was to churn and reorganize. Every new senior leader (usually hired from the outside) believed that they should mark their territory by reorganizing their corner of the company. Because turnover was quite high among senior leaders at the company, it seemed to be in a constant state of reorganization.

When I came along, there was a new CEO in place who was convinced that reorganizing was the best path forward, despite the fact that huge swaths of the company were already suffering from reorg anxiety and fatigue, and now they were going to be plunged into more uncertainty.

The reorg took over two years and involved multiple layoffs spread months apart. The initial announcement and every subsequent change created and exacerbated a massive amount of fear, uncertainty, and doubt. From that moment forward, nearly everyone I ran into at the company was in some form of self-protection or disengagement. Plans were put on hold because no one was certain that any team would still even be there in a week or if we ourselves would even have jobs (you can't operate as a team when your teammates are being reassigned or are vanishing before your eyes almost weekly). Political showmanship was at an all-time high. No one was getting anything done, but managers were sure good at making it appear otherwise . . . in a PowerPoint sort of way.

Many of those put in charge of who to keep and who to let go were already drops of poison in the organization. The result is that many compassionate leaders were let go. Talented workers, who loved those leaders, left on their own shortly thereafter. Many of those left behind suffered a high personal cost. Some went on leave of absence for mental health—and often left the company afterwards. Others left to escape the anxiety from uncertainty. Morale was very low.

All of us want stable ground to stand on and we do our best work this way. Imagine how difficult it would be for an artist to paint a beautiful mural if they were standing on rickety scaffolding. Our prefrontal cortex is short-circuited by our amygdala when we feel we are in danger. If the environment in our companies is toxic and uncertain, we are paying our employees to walk around in corporate Hunger Games rather than innovating for the growth of the company. Even if they *want* to innovate, the amygdala will make the task nearly impossible. So, the first pillar of a good world to work in is stability.

Leaders must do their best to shield employees from uncertainty and avoid doing things that create instability. This means creating systems and environments where changing work is brought to stable teams, not where teams are constantly reformed to suit the changing work. It means making and keeping pledges of stability for team formation. Allowing teammates to get to know and trust each other long enough to make it all the way through Tuckman's forming, storming, norming, and performing phases. This is a win-win situation. Leaders who leave teams to mature in this way will likely experience increased performance and innovation from their employees.

Personal Stability

One of the facets of organizational instability we touched on is the risk of being laid off or let go. This becomes especially risky the closer one comes to retirement age. From Maslow's Hierarchy of Needs (see page 75), we know that personal safety is second only to air, food, and water for human beings. In the United States, losing your job means also losing your healthcare insurance, which plunges us to the lowest level of Maslow's model. The stakes are incredibly high for people, easily reaching fight or flight response territory. To make matters worse, companies have been dangerously toying with employees' personal stability for decades in some Jenga game of seeing how many things they can take away without the entire system falling to pieces. Consider the ways companies have been treating employees over the decades:

- They lobby politicians to keep unions from forming/labor

laws weak and minimum wages low.
- They've ended pension and retirement programs, replacing them with "fend for yourself" retirement strategies like 401Ks.
- They lobby against universal healthcare.
- At the first sign of jeopardy for missing quarterly profit projections, executives cut perks and lay off employees in large numbers. Companies often reward this behavior by giving obscene bonuses to those executives or use the money saved for stock buybacks.
- They readily replace employees with automation or outsource work to developing nations.

Collectively, these actions repeatedly scream one message at employees very loudly: **"You don't matter. We don't owe you anything, least of all security."**

It appears that employees have finally heard the message. As I mentioned, the world is in the midst of a large labor backlash some have called "the great resignation." Record numbers of employees are resigning from their jobs and going elsewhere. The media coverage seems mixed about the various reasons for these departures. Low pay and the inability to work remotely full-time are at the top of most lists, but I think those explanations are all symptoms of a much larger problem: *employees are simply done believing that companies and their leaders care about them.*

The data backs my theory up. A recent study[47] revealed that the number one reason by far that employees are leaving their companies in droves is toxic culture. It is ten times more likely to predict departure than compensation. According to the study, the five attributes of toxic culture are (in order): disrespectful, noninclusive, unethical, cutthroat, and abusive. Disrespectful breaks down into lack of consideration, courtesy, and dignity for others.

---

[47] Donald Sull et al., "Why Every Leader Needs to Worry about Toxic Culture," MITSloan Management Review, last modified March 16, 2022, accessed April 6, 2022, https://sloanreview.mit.edu/article/why-every-leader-needs-to-worry-about-toxic-culture/.

If you want a competitive edge in the market, there is no better time than now for you to create a place where employees can grow with you. That means ensuring their retirement safety, it means sharing profits, it means taking care of their healthcare, and it means taking an active interest in their wellbeing, education, and career goals. It means treating them with respect and honoring their service to your company. It also means that you do what you can to ensure they have a job even when profits ebb and flow. CEOs who have done these things in these moments have been astounded by how innovative, motivated, and frugal employees can get during hard times.

I'm not suggesting that companies go bankrupt trying to keep employees and pay them well, but many companies are not near bankruptcy. They are protecting millions—if not billions—of dollars in profit by laying employees off. If your business model depends on being able to take advantage of humans by underpaying them or treating them like expendable capital, you may want to revisit your business model.

Will it be expensive? Yes. Will it eat into profits? Yes. But I think if we're being honest, those profit margins have been maintained on borrowed time considering how long they've been increasing by reducing the benefits to employees listed above.

Taking care of employees will build loyalty. Remember, loyalty is not bought or commanded. It bounces back at you when you send it down your organization from the top. Be prepared to earn it. It took years to teach employees that they didn't matter. It'll take years to convince them that they do. Don't wait another minute to start.

Create Safety

Safety comes in many flavors. We discussed the lower Maslow levels of physiological and physical safety as they relate to stability, but safety appears at the higher levels of Belonging and Esteem as well. These are social and egocentric levels. Once we know we are fed and physically safe, we can begin focusing on acceptance in our group and acceptance in the mirror. Leaders can create or destroy this kind of safety as well. Here are a few examples of cultural safety that leaders impact regularly.

Safety to Fail

We've touched upon the safety to fail several times already but allow me to give you a few real examples of what it looks like when that safety doesn't exist.

At one company I worked with, there was a large production failure during a holiday season. The problem was fixed quickly but even so a senior executive at the company called his leadership team into a meeting where he said, "I'm going to go around the room to each of you individually and I want you each to explain to me why I shouldn't fire you right now."

Not to state the obvious here, but that wasn't brilliant leadership in any form. It immediately created fear and infighting as each leader looked for ways to escape responsibility for the problem. It shut down the prefrontal cortexes of everyone in the room as their amygdalae jumped in with adrenaline as a response to fear and anger. People dislike experiencing these emotions. They also dislike people who they believe *caused* them, which is why loyalty and trust towards this executive went out the window instantly. Rather than learning from the failure and strengthening the systems involved, nothing positive emerged from that meeting. In fact, several talented leaders departed the company shortly thereafter.

In another example, I was coaching a VP for a large financial tech company. He was frustrated that his leadership team continually reported status on projects as green (on schedule, no problems) then, at the last minute, they would flip red. In my field we call these watermelon projects—green on the outside, red on the inside.

He said, "I want them to tell me sooner. I may be able to help them get back on track if they let me know they're struggling. But by the time they flip red, it's too late and we're in evasive maneuvers."

"When was the last time you took one of these managers to task for something negative?" I asked.

"About thirty minutes ago during my staff meeting," he said.

"I think I may know what's wrong," I told him.

This VP wanted to be told what was wrong, but because he continually demonstrated that it wasn't safe to fail by getting visibly upset every time he was given bad news, his direct reports were playing a game called project chicken. Everyone reports green until the first person cannot avoid it any longer and flips to red. Then, since they all now have someone to blame for their projects being delayed, everyone else flips red too and points to some dependency on the poor person who just lost the game.

This VP's direct reports weren't the only ones affected, of course; just imagine how their anxiety affected each of their teams.

To change the behavior in this case, I had the VP announce to his team that he realized the error of his ways and that his reactions were teaching the team not to tell him about project risks earlier. He stressed that the team needed to have small failures *faster* rather than large failures slower. As David Marquet says in *Turn the Ship Around!*, "A little rudder far from the rocks is better than a lot of rudder close to the rocks."

To aid the company in its new approach, instead of red/yellow/green, I had them instill a different measure called the fist of five. At staff meetings, the leader would ask the team on the count of three to hold up the number of fingers, one to five, that represented their confidence in their projects being on track—everyone at the same second, so no one's finger count would influence anyone else's. Privately, I counseled the leader to praise any team member who showed the courage to display anything less than five fingers. That was to be his moment to demonstrate safety to the group *and* offer to support the project earlier.

Things improved very quickly for that team, but I want to stress that it wasn't *just* the fist of five that made the difference.

It was the leader admitting his mistake and promising to do better. This was, itself, a demonstration of safety to fail. The leader was demonstrating vulnerability by owning his own failures. I suspect that his public praise of lower finger counts also went a long way towards creating safety.

There is an old story, perhaps lore, of a senior IBM leader whose mistake cost the company $10 million. He was summoned to his boss's office for a meeting. When he arrived, he told his boss, "I just want to say that I'm sorry and I've come prepared with my resignation."

"Resign? Why would I want you resign?" his boss responded. "Your education just cost me ten million dollars!"

I have hammered on this point several times throughout this book, but it bears repeating here: You will not innovate if your employees are only willing to do things that will not fail. To counteract this, leadership from the top needs to do more than simply make it safe to fail. They need to encourage and celebrate fast failure as much as they do the wins. After all, you now know another way that won't work. Perhaps that gives you a leg up on your competition who are about to spend a lot of money going down that incorrect path. As Peter Senge, author of *The Fifth Discipline* notes, "In the long run, the only sustainable source of competitive advantage is your organization's ability to learn faster than your competition."

Safety Not to Know

Once we reach a certain level at our jobs, it can begin to feel as if we're always supposed to know the answer. We believe that if we say, "I don't know," others will be thinking, "What are we paying you for?" This is especially true in highly competitive companies where it seems that even the receptionists are required to have degrees from an Ivy League university. This can lead to imposter's syndrome where employees feel that they don't belong with their peers because they simply don't have an answer every time. If we don't feel that it's safe not to know, it can be tempting to lie our way through the answer. If we do this enough, we begin to believe our own bullshit. Suddenly we're defending a substandard answer that we invented instead of hearing other people's responses.

When we can say, "I don't know," we can also say, "let's find out!" right afterwards. When we force people to stand behind a position they don't feel strongly about, conversely, we chase rabbits down holes, wasting a lot of time and money.

Safety to Speak Up

I often hear leaders with the best intentions implore their teams to speak up by saying, "My door is open. Please feel free to let me know what's on your mind." Inherent in this approach is a belief that those team members feel safe to speak up. An open door means nothing if no one wants to use it. Intentionally or not, many leaders and companies have sent a clear message that it's not safe to speak up. Perhaps the last person who did so was passed up for a promotion, received a less than satisfactory performance review, or was laid off. Even if these outcomes were genuinely unrelated to the speaking up, if the *belief* is that they were connected, the damage is done, and it spreads.

When thinking about whether it's safe to speak up in your organization, remember to look at the actions not the words. You can count on the fact that your employees will. This includes not just the bad behavior that is reported but goes on uncorrected, but also the bad behavior that is outright rewarded. What messages are you sending to the organization through your actions or inactions? This is a crucial foundation of the safety to speak up.

Create Connection

Some time ago, I was at a company where a team I was working with was struggling with too much tech debt. They were unable to get it under control because their product organization kept piling new feature work onto their backlogs with organizational pressure to get it done quickly. And when the team raised a concern to their manager, the response was, "Show me the data."

On the surface that seems like a defensible request. But what I noticed—and what the leader didn't—was how the team members' shoulders all fell when he said that. They were deflated. As they saw it, they were screaming about being overworked—so much so that they were patching things together with duct tape and bailing wire. Instead of getting help from their manager, they were getting more work. They had to *prove* they needed help. They also heard "I don't trust you" loud and clear. I began hearing grumblings like, "If he would just come down from his ivory tower for five seconds, he'd see we were telling the truth."

What a squandered opportunity to create connection! In fact, it was worse than that. It didn't just *not create* connection, it actively created *disconnection*.

The marines have a term I love called "eyeball leadership." You must spend time with people and teams you lead if you want to be a successful leader. By showing up and doing the right things (mostly asking questions and listening), you create connection. That connection is a major deposit into the trust jar, as Brené Brown calls it. As I mentioned before, credibility is a multiplier. Listening to employees regularly is a great way to build it.

When I coach leaders on this, they often tell me, "I just don't have time." We then go through their calendar together and discover that it is full of meetings they don't need to be in. Sometimes, they've injected themselves into a process as an approval bottleneck because they don't trust their employees. Sometimes their calendars are filled with death-by-status-update meetings where the Peacocks in the organization are trying to strut. Often, the lack of safety in an organization can fill a leader's calendar with meetings where employees run every little step past the boss for approval.

Examine your calendar for what to say no to in order to create the time for more eyeball leadership. What underlying toxicity in your organization is filling it with unnecessary meetings and preventing you from this kind of leadership?

Create Clarity

Clarity is kind.

– Brené Brown

Clarity of roles and processes are essential elements of a sane organization. This clarity can exist even when the overall environment is chaotic—in fact, some of the most chaotic and high-pressure jobs have clarity of role and process. First responder, military, air traffic control, and hospital emergency rooms all have process and role clarity. That clarity is what grounds people when the world around them seems unsteady. Your job as a leader is to create—and empower others to create—clarity.

Many of the stressed-out professionals I coach are suffering from a lack of clarity in their workplace. If these companies were a professional football team, the players would be banging into each other on the field, running the wrong direction, holding onto the ball too long, or not receiving a pass when it comes their way. This is no way to play and it's certainly no way to win.

The true art is to create just enough clarity to feel held by it but not so much that we feel choked. I call it an art because there are many subtle ways to do this wrong. Create too much constraint and process and you strangle a team's ability to innovate. Create not enough and they will get in their own and each other's way requiring heroic effort to accomplish the simplest of value delivery. I'm often surprised by the number of companies I work with that are proud of their teams' ability to perform diving catches without once questioning why their organizations are operating in a way that makes these kinds of catches necessary so often. Sure, reward the good catch but go find the bad throw!

Clarity is more than just nicely written job descriptions or an internal wiki with a series of processes to follow. The reason these are not enough is because the circumstances on the ground day-to-day are always evolving and testing them. They are living and breathing artifacts that require constant attention.

Clarity of roles doesn't mean that change and adaptation cannot happen. A team could rotate the role of production support to different team members every other week, for example. What clarity would require here is not that the person or people in the role remain the same but that it be *clear to everyone who is in it*.

A word of caution here. Some of the most dysfunctional organizations I've worked with were created by executives who rarely left their offices and didn't have a clue what most of the employees in the organization actually did day-to-day. It's a leader's job to empower teams to create clarity if at all possible. Be wary of becoming a Chess Master leader who tries to create clarity *for* teams. Instead, when a lack of clarity is identified, ask yourself if the clarity is needed from someone at your level or if the teams should be able to create it themselves with your encouragement and support. Whether it be process or role clarity, the people doing the work are often the ones in the best position to determine how it gets done and who does what. This speaks to Agile's principle: the best architectures, requirements, and designs emerge from self-organizing teams.

Create Purpose

Perhaps one of the largest fundamental disagreements one can get into in my line of work is that of the purpose of business. As I mentioned before, I often hear it argued that the purpose of business is to make money. I believe that those who make this argument are mistaking purpose with need. The human body cannot survive without blood and oxygen, but it would be overly reductive to describe the purpose of the human body as creating blood and using oxygen. They are certainly needed functions, but they are not its purpose.

Seen in this way, you may understand how I might not be surprised that an executive onstage at an all-hands event, droning on for twenty minutes about how much money the company has made in the previous quarter or year, doesn't move anyone in the room. Most of the people in that audience are likely getting the same paycheck regardless of the company's money supply, while the executive onstage is imagining his new yacht with his stock bonus. Even if the employees are sharing in the monetary success, they rarely connect their own performance with that success in a meaningful way at most large companies.

The problem with thinking the purpose of business is to make money is that it can turn you into a mindless (and some would argue, heartless) leader that senselessly chews through natural and human resources (human beings). If you believe the purpose of business is to make money, you may have gotten your yacht, but you've missed the boat. You haven't created anything *actionable* for your employees and you've potentially sabotaged your company's long-term success for short-term gain. Yes, you need enough money to keep things growing and going, but when it becomes the obsessive navigation metric used at every crossroad, it will lead the company down the wrong path.

As a leader, you are in control of creating a purpose for employees to rally for, and that purpose must have a personal connection to the people working for you. At some level, employees must believe that the work they do for you contributes to a higher purpose than just making money. Whether your company writes accounting software or designs dental equipment, people who work for you should be passionate about getting numbers right or helping people look their best and chew without pain. You create that passion, and you attract people to work for you who share that passion with you.

The fastest way to destroy that passion? By boiling everything down to the bottom line—especially when most of your employees won't be sharing in the wealth.

DEEPER DIVE

The Infinite Game by Simon Sinek

Create Impact

In 2017, my mom was living with me and my partner. She had been diagnosed with cancer and dementia. As part of her cancer treatment, she was radiated in the brain. The radiation made her dementia much worse almost overnight, which, we were told, was a rare side effect.

Suddenly, my mom needed full-time care, so my partner put his education and career on hold and took care of her during the day while I went to work. But as her dementia worsened, it became clear very quickly that my partner couldn't do it alone—if you've ever cared for anyone with dementia or Alzheimer's, you know what I mean—so I took a leave of absence from work for the final four to six weeks of her life until she passed away in our home.

After my mom's service and my bereavement period, I returned to work, anxious to roll up my sleeves and get back to it—as a distraction from the loss, if nothing else. In my first team meeting back, I asked, "So what did I miss?" My coworker, Dave, interrupted me and said, "Before we get back into it, let me just say that we missed you here while you were gone. Our conversations were not as rich and our solutions not as thorough without you."

It was striking to me how good it felt to hear that. It reinvigorated me by reminding me why I do the work. It made me want to roll up my sleeves and dive right back into it. That was the moment I understood impact.

While purpose is a larger objective for an organization, I think of impact as more personal. You may be wondering what you can do as a leader to create impact and avoid its destruction. Have you ever had a job where you weren't quite sure why they hired you? Perhaps the skills you had were not in demand on the team, perhaps the things they had you doing seemed like busywork. Maybe you and a coworker seem to be stepping on each other's feet constantly. These scenarios are all poor leadership outcomes and lead to a lack of impact for all involved.

If you throw money and staff at problems as a first choice or reorganize your company without being thoughtful and strategic, you risk fragmenting the work, creating territorial conflicts, and decreasing the chances that any individual will feel they are making an impact. To be crystal clear here, I'm not advising that you keep a skeleton crew so your employees are making their impact through repeated diving catches. I'm just advising against the opposite situation where thoughtless hiring and (re)organization will cause there to be a saturation of people all running for the same ball in the same part of the field.

Whether someone will feel that they make an impact or not is dependent upon many factors, but you do have the ability to create an environment where people have an increased chance to make an impact. Or you can destroy that possibility by being careless about who you hire, how many you hire, and how you structure your organization. Empowered teams foster empowered team members, and empowered team members can make an impact.

Impact comes from a person's ability to contribute knowledge and experience, not just effort. So, remember to give employees the space, time, and opportunities to contribute in ways you may not have originally hired them for. Oh, and like my friend Dave, make sure you let someone know if they make an impact that you notice.

The Power Is Yours

Some leaders seem to rail against the idea of self-organizing teams because they think it means self-*managing* (spoiler alert: it doesn't). The fact is, leading others is a very powerful position. It's just not a power over *people*. It's a power over the *environment* that people work in. As a leader, you might oversee thousands of decisions that affect the world your employees exist inside of while they are at work. Everything from company policies to compensation to how frustrating the system is to work in and how safe it is to criticize it in the interest of making it better. Your employees create the products and services your customers want to buy. You create the environment that attracts and retains those employees to do so. That environment can contain stability, safety, connection, clarity, purpose, and impact or it can be lacking those things. The power is yours.

CHAPTER 14: TOXIC LEADERSHIP ARCHETYPES REVISITED

Change is good, but you go first.

– Unknown

Courage is knowing it might hurt and doing it anyway. Stupidity is the same. And that is why life is hard.

– Jeremy Goldberg

As you were reading through the list of toxic leadership archetypes in Chapter 1, you may have spotted yourself in one of them. It takes a lot of courage, self-awareness, and humility to do so, but several of my early readers had this experience. Refer to Chapter 1 for a refresher of each type and see if you can spot any of the behaviors in yourself.

If you think you have a blind spot about your own behavior as a leader, reach out to people who care about you enough to tell you the truth and provide them the safety to tell you if you behave like one or more of these archetypes. These should be people who observe you as a leader at work. Friends and partners likely don't see you this way. Even peers who are also leaders can be challenging for this purpose as they often don't see the way you treat employees or may lead just like you and have the same blind spots.

People who you *used* to lead but don't currently are the absolute best source for this feedback. These are folks you no longer have any control over and who, when invited, may be more candid with you about what it was like to work for you. Most toxic leaders will not be able to get this kind of feedback from people they currently lead without a coach like me in between. The trust and safety are usually not there.

You may find that you exhibit behaviors from several archetypes, but no one can settle on a single archetype for you, and this is fine. All the archetype behaviors are toxic to teams; you don't have to exhibit every behavior from a singular archetype to be a problem. It's more important that you identify all of your toxic behaviors, period.

Since we're in the part of the book about becoming a better leader, it's the right place for us to revisit these archetypes with an eye on what you can do to detoxify your teams if you behave like one of them. If you happen to work for a leader with one of these archetypes, I will also offer some tips to manage up with this kind of leader.

Keep in mind that most of these archetypes are really just mindsets about leadership. Accordingly, as we address each archetype, I'm going to talk a lot about values, beliefs, and principles. The best way to figure out your mindset about leadership is to do the mindset exercise in Appendix A, so I suggest you jump there and do that now before reading on. Having put some thought into your mindset will help you more easily relate to one or more of these archetypes.

The Chess Master

Chess Master leaders believe leadership is the reward, not a responsibility, and that there is an inherent hierarchy in place. They believe that their ascendence to leadership is because they have the best answers and, therefore, people below them should follow their instructions and plans like pieces on their chess board.

How Do Chess Masters Detoxify?

If you are a Chess Master, your first steps should be to analyze where your beliefs come from. People do what makes sense to them. Which values and beliefs do you hold that make this behavior seem right to you? What would it take for you to challenge those beliefs?

As I mentioned in Chapter 1, the Chess Master type can often emerge from the culture you were raised in. If you've only experienced a societal pressure to "know your place" and honor leaders, then when you are promoted to a leadership position, you may model this hierarchical style yourself. But this is a toxic command-and-control style.

One suggestion I make for Chess Master leaders is to run experiments with the team, letting them solve problems the leader believes they themselves should own. For example, say there is a quality problem on the team. Chess Master leaders usually swoop in with new procedures and processes and quality gates in a "let me check your room before you can go out with your friends" kind of way.

I advise Chess Masters to be honest with the team, broaching the topic with something like:

> I'm usually the type to spot a problem and then solve it, but I don't think that's a healthy leadership trait and I'm working on trying to move more of the solution space over to you as a team. I've spotted a problem with quality. We've had five escaped defects for the past few releases. Do you all agree this is a problem to solve?

Once the team agrees, the next step is to ask for help:

> Ok, then what I'd like to do is try a new approach. Can I get you guys to meet up—without me at first—to discuss what might be the root cause of the problem, and then propose some suggested actions we can try, including any specific requests you have for me for ways I can support you as a leader?

This kind of frank, vulnerable request feels really awkward for most Chess Master types. If you try this approach—and I can't stress this enough—what you must do afterwards is really appreciate whatever the team comes up with. If you don't think the team's solution is complete or the right approach, instead of shooting it down, merely ask a powerful question that begins with what or how. Such as, "How will you address the problem of . . ." or "What will you do if . . ." or "How are you addressing the concern that . . ." These questions are not leading. They are coming from your experience and also a place of genuine curiosity. Yes, the team's solution must address your concerns, so advocate for those concerns (the problem) but not *your solution*. My guess is that as a Chess Master, you've been tying your value as a leader to the *solutions you create*. Instead, it's vital that you begin tying your value to *advocating for the problems you want the team to solve* instead.

If you've been Chess Mastering with your team for a long time, it may take a few attempts at this for your team to realize that you mean it and to really grab the handlebars and ride. Stick with it. Your value to your team is expressed by the barriers you clear for them using your level in the organization.

Lastly, I'd advise that Chess Masters read the book *The Motive* by Patrick Lencioni. It can help you spot your motive to be a leader and determine how that contributes to your leadership style.

Managing Up to a Chess Master

If you work for a Chess Master, it can be a very disempowering experience. You are often handed solutions and directions that they have determined without your input.

It's important to understand that Chess Masters don't realize they're having this impact. They think the value they add is in having the answer when it's really about having the question. Since Chess Masters are often culturally influenced to behave this way, however, and the root of the behavior is deeply entrenched, they usually don't shake out of the behavior just because they're made aware of it. Even so, that doesn't mean it isn't useful to begin there. So, I usually advise employees of Chess Masters to raise awareness of how disempowered they feel. Something like:

> I've noticed that whenever the team has encountered an issue, you tend to give us the solution rather than let us wrestle with the problem. When that happens, we feel disempowered. Like a set of hands for you instead of a team full of brains. I'm wondering what it would take for you to feel comfortable letting us take a stab at solving it? As a team, we'd still like your feedback on whatever we come up with to make sure it addresses the problem completely, but we would like to be more involved in the solution. Would that be ok?

Chess Masters who can't let go of this behavior will never be good leaders, so your only real solution is to leave. Just make sure that on the way out, you respectfully convey the reason you're leaving. You may be the fifth employee to leave this leader who pointed to this as the reason. This greatly helps coaches like me. When we get called in to help, we're met by a leader who's desperate to change rather than one fighting us through denial.

The Peacock and The Ladder Climber

I'm going to cover these two archetypes together since they are both quite similar to each other. The only real difference is that

Peacocks are usually more covert about their desire to move up while Ladder Climbers will tell anyone who will listen.

Peacocks do strut their stuff upwardly, but their downward focus is on getting teams to help them be promoted under the guise of solving problems for the organization. They want to move up the org as a primary goal and spend a lot of time—their own and that of their teams—preparing data to show how well things are going and carefully avoiding things that aren't going well. Peacocks usually share a trait of Chess Masters as well: They think they know what's best. The difference is that is it's usually what's best for *them*, not the team or the organization. Peacocks and Ladder Climbers spend a lot more of their time with their bosses than they do with their employees.

How Do Peacocks and Ladder Climbers Detoxify?

Like the Chess Master, you Peacocks or Ladder Climbers should complete the mindset exercise in Appendix A. This will give you a solid understanding of the values and beliefs you hold that make your behaviors make sense to you. You, too, should read *The Motive* by Patrick Lencioni to understand your priorities towards climbing versus leading. One concept that is useful for Peacocks and Ladder Climbers is this:

> The best way to get promoted is to be pushed up from below rather than by pulling yourself up.

This feels very unnatural for Peacocks and Ladder Climbers. You may be operating under these beliefs:

- If you want it, you have to reach for it.
- Nothing good will come unless you take it.
- You make your own luck.

Beliefs like these make great motivational cat posters but often cause people to believe that others are there to be stepped on to get a bit higher. It may seem very counterintuitive to a Peacock that being pushed up to a new height is the preferred way to get there because they think others admire their grit, focus, and determination. But pulling yourself into your next promotion is a lonely way to succeed.

I once worked with an amazing leader who led a couple hundred adoring employees. They would have done just about anything for him. The CTO announced this leader's promotion to VP in front of the entire group of hundreds of people. Everyone got on their feet to applaud.

You know someone deserved a promotion when you're hearing the troops say, "It's about time! What took so long?!?" If you're seeing eye rolls and hearing, "Why him?" you know there's trouble. Too often, this is the fate of Peacocks. Don't be this person. And if you're a Peacock who's thinking, "Who cares what they think? It's *my* career!" Then I'd argue that you are the kind of toxic leader we're all working on ridding our organizations of. You're not trying to dominate at a game of Monopoly. There are real human beings whose lives are impacted greatly by your style, and if your approach to getting a promotion is "take no prisoners," you are misguided.

Peacocks are greatly enabled and encouraged by the culture in their companies. If the company rewards high performers with promotions, it can spawn Peacock and Ladder Climber infestations. If you're a Peacock but don't want to be, and you work for a company that rewards Peacock behavior, you are essentially an alcoholic who works as a bartender and need to find another company that thinks of leadership correctly.

Detoxifying yourself as a Peacock or Ladder Climber is more of an internal journey that brings your motives, values, and beliefs to the forefront. What if you made it all the way to CEO but had the respect of no one? What if you sit on a throne ruling over a kingdom of people who dislike you so much that they're just counting the days until your fall, or maybe actively conspiring to bring it about? What if you're surrounded by people who tell you what you want to hear while the rest of those you lead know you're an emperor who wears no clothes? If these outcomes aren't acceptable to you, then it's important that you move away from being a Peacock or Ladder Climber as much as possible. You will only be a leader if people are behind you. It won't be because you got a title that made you higher than others in an org chart. That just put you in charge and made you a manager.

If you are unable to figure out your drive for title and position at all costs, don't be afraid to enlist the help of a good therapist. There's nothing wrong with title and position, but those who want it for the sake of having it will find that, just like money, it's a means to an end, not the end itself. A leadership coach can help you spot toxic behaviors with your teams and help you find healthy replacement behaviors. They can also help you find ways to challenge the beliefs, values, and principles that make up your mindset about leadership (again, see Appendix A), but they shouldn't attempt to replace a good therapist.

Managing Up to a Peacock or Ladder Climber

This is a rough kind of boss to have. The first thing you must accept is that if your boss is one of these archetypes, they likely have a keen sense of loyalty and disloyalty. Loyalty is usually a value for these archetypes, and they have learned to rid themselves of any employees they deem as disloyal because only loyal employees will support their conquest goals. If you want to keep your job, you'll need to make a show of your loyalty. They don't think they need to do *anything* to earn *your* loyalty. They think they should have it because . . . well . . . they think they are entitled to it.

Be careful not to fall into traps around loyalty. I've seen the incentives for loyalty created by Peacocks lead good people into behaving poorly towards their peers in the interest of keeping their jobs or maybe being promoted themselves. I've also seen people completely sell their souls to gain favor with Peacocks only to be seen as weak by the Peacock and kicked into the pit "This is SPARTA!" style.

It is *very* hard to win with Peacocks and Ladder Climbers. These are two of the leader types that I usually just advise that employees get away from since their motives are so toxic, self-centered, and misaligned from their employees. It's you versus their narcissistic pursuits, and you will rarely stand a chance.

The Micromanager

Micromanagers are perfectionists who believe that no one seems to care about doing a good job. They often have the belief that "if you want something done well, you have to do it yourself." Perfectionists struggle in their own lives with meeting their own impossible standards. It can lead to procrastination and imposter syndrome.

When people who have these issues get put into leadership positions, their dysfunctional and unhelpful behaviors get transferred to their teams. These leaders feel they must be involved in every single detail of every decision, hence, the birth of a Micromanager. Chances are very high that these behaviors show up outside of work as well. They are usually helicopter parents and nagging spouses. Like most of these toxic archetypes, these behaviors stem from values, beliefs, and principles—some of which were instilled very early in life.

How Do Micromanagers Detoxify?

Recognizing that the felt need to micromanage is coming from an internal bar of your own idea of "correct" or "done" is the first step in moving away from micromanagement. Micromanagers need to become experts at focusing on outcomes rather than outputs. It's important that you are clear about what success looks like and when you're expecting it but remain indifferent about how that success is reached. You cannot move the goalposts for your team when they meet the success criteria you outlined, or you will sow distrust. Iteration is fine. But celebrate the success first. For example:

> Great! This definitely meets the criteria I gave you and I'm happy! Now that I'm looking at it finished, I'm realizing that there is something additional we should consider. [Outline what's new]. Do you agree that adding this would be valuable?

The hardest thing for Micromanagers to do is accept something that they feel is not perfect. As a perfectionist, you'll tend to circle around perfection at the expense of progress. You'll demand your team spend 80 percent of their time honing the last 20 percent of the work without recognizing that you're the only one who probably cares about the details you're pushing for. This isn't an argument for mediocrity, but it is a reminder that one person's mediocre is another's perfect, and perfectionists usually have a big calibration problem on this scale.

Confirmation bias will also come into play for you as a Micromanager. You will tend to notice and pay more attention to any time the team's solutions didn't hit the mark but underplay or miss the times they knocked it out of the park. This feeds your narrative that you need to step in and micromanage. Here's the curse of Micromanagers: *you create your own reality*. The more you step *in* because you believe the team can't do it without you, the more the team will step *out* because, in their mind, there is just no pleasing you. The team's disengagement will only serve to confirm to you that you need to step in, and the vicious cycle begins.

Because micromanagement is often rooted in perfectionism and distrust—which are personal battles—it's important that you work with a therapist and a coach to address those issues. The worksheet in Appendix A can help identify the core beliefs that are worth examining in these settings. Again, it is highly unlikely that this micromanagement behavior is only surfacing at work, so examining the root cause could benefit you in many other facets of your life.

Managing Up to a Micromanager

Like working for a Chess Master, working for a Micromanager feels very disempowering. They are usually very focused on *how* you solve problems at the expense of clearly describing *what* the problem is and what outcome they are looking for. It's important that you communicate any feelings you have. Tell them that you're having a difficult time staying engaged with the work because the goalposts either aren't clear or are moving as you reach them. Most Micromanagers secretly know they're micromanaging. They've probably been told by spouses, partners, children, and previous teams. They usually don't *want* to micromanage but don't know how to stop.

Since most micromanagement stems from a lack of trust, ask your Micromanager boss what it would take for you to earn their trust in solving the problem. Ask for very specific true/false criteria. Don't accept something like, "Well, I'd trust you more if the solutions you came up with looked more professional." That is very subjective. Instead, ask for objective criteria for success and get an agreement that if you meet those criteria, you will have put a coin in the trust jar. You want to set up situations where the problem definition belongs to them, and the solution belongs to you. To counter their temptation to succumb to confirmation bias, continually remind them of the times that you met or exceeded their expectations.

Working for a Micromanager becomes much easier when they have acknowledged that they want to change; then you can offer them opportunities to work on it. But silence in the face of micromanagement will only cause them to double down and make it worse. So, if you're unwilling to manage up with them and/or they seem unwilling to acknowledge their problem, it may be time to move on. Again, if you do move on, be honest with them about why. Among other things, it makes my job as a coach much easier.

The Invertebrate

Invertebrates are everyone's friend and no one's leader. They avoid confrontation like the plague and hope that problems on the team will just go away if they aren't talked about. While I don't think leaders need to be authoritarians who are socially distant from team members, I do think every leader will encounter situations that require a "boss hat." There are behavioral issues on the team that sometimes need addressing. There are times when the team needs their leader to have a spine on their behalf when dealing with people outside of their organization. Invertebrates let their teams down in these moments.

How Do Invertebrates Detoxify?

If you're an Invertebrate, it often stems from a psychological need for acceptance and/or a fear of conflict. Most Invertebrates I've worked with have long personal histories that point to this as a coping strategy. As children, it may have been a great survival mechanism to lay low in the face of conflict, however, as a leader this will not serve you. Therapy can help you turn and confront the ghosts you may be running from in this area. From a leadership perspective, the key traits you're going for are being *confident and assertive*. To you, this may feel like I'm asking you to be an asshole, but I assure you I'm not. You can be confident and assertive without being a jerk about it.

Before Dr. Phil became a bit too much like Jerry Springer for my taste, he once said that, in his line of work, he was often suddenly confronted with quite unpredictable behavior. One thing he repeatedly told himself is that no matter what the other person does, he can handle it. So, a key part of Invertebrates growing a spine is learning how to handle unpredictable behavior and high stakes conversations. The best way I know for this to happen is by reading the book *Crucial Conversations* and even contacting the company that wrote the book, Crucial Learning, to take a course on it. Another great book on conflict management is *The Anatomy of Peace* by The Arbinger Institute. These kinds of resources will give you the tools to become more confident when conversations involve high stakes, high emotions, and differing opinions. The more you flex these muscles, the more you will begin seeing these situations like Dr. Phil described—with a confidence that you can handle it. Then you'll be less likely to bury your head in the sand when they arise. Your team will appreciate it.

If you simply cannot imagine ever being comfortable with being confident and assertive either towards or on behalf of one of your employees, you really need to rethink your decision to go into leadership. No one follows someone who cannot act with confidence and assertiveness. Hold onto your compassion and desire to connect. Those are strengths for leadership. But they cannot come at the expense of confidence and assertiveness. Your desire to be everyone's friend is fine. Just make sure you're the kind of friend who can deliver hard truths with candor and compassion.

Managing Up to an Invertebrate

If you have an Invertebrate as a boss, it can leave you feeling helpless—especially in the face of team or organizational dysfunction. While it can feel empowering when you think your leader is leaving you alone to do your work, that feeling can quickly evaporate the moment you realize that they're actually leaving you alone to fend for yourself. Often, we don't realize we have an Invertebrate boss until we need them and find them with their head in the sand. In this moment, it's important that you privately let them know that you really need them to step into the situation and help.

One of the stories that Invertebrates tell themselves to feel better about hiding is that you don't really need their help and they would only be getting in the way if they stepped in. Take that story away from them by telling them you need them. Remember to do this privately as it will feel less like being called out for weakness that way. If the letdown is being felt by the entire team, have each team member privately ask the Invertebrate for help in the matter rather than teaming up on them. Remember, Invertebrates run from confrontation. If they feel like they're being confronted about their lack of confrontation, they'll retreat from that as well.

Be specific about what you need from the Invertebrate. What you may be expecting from them might be a lot easier for them to do than what they were imagining you needed, so remove that anxiety and specify exactly what a win would look like for you from them. You truly do need to manage up with Invertebrates. Just be careful not to do their jobs for them. Not only can you get into hot water for acting like a manager without being one, you also further convince the Invertebrate that their noninvolvement was the right choice.

The Drill Sergeant

Drill Sergeants believe that people need to be told what to do and what not to do. They are like Micromanagers and Chess Masters on steroids—literally. While you may be imagining a male in this archetype, let me assure you that Drill Sergeants can also be female.

The beliefs that underlie a Drill Sergeant's behaviors are often a need for process and order. Like Micromanagers, this is usually deeply rooted in childhood. It was how they were parented or, perhaps, a reaction to having *no order* during their childhood. Some Drill Sergeants were literally former military and are just following leadership behaviors they were shown during boot camp. I do want to be clear, however, that most of the *best* leadership behavior I've seen often comes from current and former leaders in the military, so this isn't meant to be a criticism of military leadership.

How Do Drill Sergeants Detoxify?

Like the other archetypes, overcoming the need for order and, sometimes, submission from others can require the assistance of a good therapist using the beliefs, values, and principles identified in Appendix A as a roadmap for the exploration. As a Drill Sergeant, you are likely feared and reviled behind your back. People comply until they cannot or will not tolerate your strictness anymore. You may see these people as quitters or people who can't stomach real work or some other framing that allows you to see yourself and your ways as superior.

You probably have a belief that demonstrating power and control is what true leadership looks like. You're wrong. You aren't leading people, you're the coachman with a whip sitting behind a team of unwilling horses. You're acting like a leader from the early nineteenth century. It, arguably, may have had a place back then. That place ended a century ago. There is a very old saying that goes, "A man convinced against his will is of his same opinion still." When you have convinced someone to agree with you or to follow your lead without coercion, you are leading. When they follow because they're being commanded to, you are managing.

My advice for Drill Sergeant types is to read the Deeper Dives below. Drill Sergeants will definitely want a leadership coach who works with them to instill new beliefs and changed behaviors. As with the other archetypes, if you're leading this way at work, you're probably leading this way everywhere else, probably with the same resentment from others. Do not fall into the Drill Sergeant trap of wearing this resentment like a badge of honor. Don't think, "They'll thank me one day." It won't happen. Instead, you'll be the subject of someone's book on toxic leadership someday, ahem, or the focus of the discussion in your kid's therapy or with your marriage counselor.

Managing Up to a Drill Sergeant

If you work for a Drill Sergeant—especially one who is unaware of it or is disinterested in changing—you are likely counting the days until you leave. The best advice I have for managing up to a Drill Sergeant is to use their desire for order against them. Explain that their constant . . . attention . . . to your every move is causing a great deal of disorder with the work. Introduce the idea of what a "good soldier" looks like. If you can get them to agree that the best kind of soldier (employee) is one who can think on their own and devise their own solutions to problems, then you may be able to back them into a definition of leadership that looks more twenty-first century.

Their desire for order and obedience is usually in service of some goal of the company or their own boss. So, it may be important for your Drill Sergeant to get the message somehow that achieving those goals can't come at the expense of burning through employees. I've sometimes had success reminding Drill Sergeants that part of their responsibilities to the company as leaders is ensuring that employee turnover is low. That is just as important, if not more important, than whatever perceived goal they're pursuing for the company.

> ### DEEPER DIVE
> *Leaders Eat Last* by Simon Sinek
> *Team of Teams* by Stanley McChrystal

The Data Freak

Data Freaks are uncomfortable with uncertainty and cling to data in an attempt to rid themselves of it. Their obsession for data usually causes trust issues with employees who feel pressured to prove obvious facts.

How Do Data Freaks Detoxify?

If you're a data freak, your biggest blind spot will be caused by confirmation bias. You'll easily recall the times (and, arguably, in a very skewed fashion) where data saved the day. You'll ignore or minimize the times that it led you astray or turned into a waste of time to collect. You'll remember the data that you collected that informed your brilliant decision while ignoring the luck of that success and, perhaps, a data point you didn't think to collect that ended up being the one that mattered the most. It is ironic, but not surprising, that the biggest strength *and weakness* of the Data Freak is the data. Once the ego gets involved, confirmation bias takes over.

Your first task is to start being more honest with yourself about the ways you may be feigning a motive of using data to *get it right* while actually using it to *be right*. Your tendency might be to use data to construct a plan, then follow that plan. This is fine if your teams are building something complicated like a bridge. It's a terrible idea if your teams are building something complex like software. The latter is best served by experimentation, not planning. Data is emergent in complex work and can be virtuous in an experiment but when you use it to try to pretend that a problem is complicated when it's really complex, you make your employees' lives a living hell. Study the Cynefin framework in Chapter 4 and read up on it elsewhere too.

Get a clear understanding of where the usefulness of data begins and ends with various types of work. Make a real commitment to release the need for data before action in every circumstance. Try to find places where your team can do short experiments and become comfortable with those experiments "failing." Become an expert at post-mortems to learn from those failures. That too is data, but its aim is more actionable and strikes a balance between too much planning and not enough.

Managing Up to a Data Freak

If you work for a Data Freak, it can be difficult to get them to let go of their belief that having data is always better. Introduce them to the Cynefin framework and explore how the different kinds of work in the model lend themselves to having varying amounts of data. Often, Data Freaks have never considered that there even *are* various kinds of work. If your work is simple, complex, or chaotic, you have a stronger argument that having the data before you move is counterproductive. If your work is complicated, the Data Freak has a stronger leg to stand on for collecting the data. Your approach then is to make sure that you collect only the data that is and will be useful. Data Freaks can be addicted to data and want to measure everything that is measurable. Introduce them to this quote from John Doerr, author of *Measure What Matters*: "We must realize—and act on the realization—that if we try to focus on everything, we focus on nothing." Maybe introduce them to the book as well.

The Bottom Liner

Bottom Liners are leaders who overly focus on the bottom line. Everything boils down to numbers. This telegraphs to employees very clearly that they are just a part of those numbers, not human beings with lives, goals, ideas, and brains. Bottom Liners are the worst at cultivating loyalty because they exude its opposite.

How Do Bottom Liners Detoxify?

If you're a Bottom Liner and want to rid yourself of the fixation, remind yourself that losing employees and their productivity is also detrimental to the bottom line. In fact, it impacts it far greater than most people realize. High turnover and low performance hurt the bottom line full-stop. Your fixation on the bottom line is causing those behaviors in employees. The paradox is that the tighter you hold on to the bottom line, the worse it gets—especially for facets of it that involve human beings. As the saying goes, if you love something, set it free. Motivated, happy employees who feel cared for will return the favor with higher performance, more innovative solutions, and more dedication. All of those will *increase the bottom line*. So it's not that I want you to ignore the bottom line, it's that I want you to see it as an outcome that is positively impacted by your ability to care about those in your charge. And I mean care about them *more* than the bottom line.

Managing Up to a Bottom Liner

If you work for a Bottom Liner, you'll want to make sure you introduce them to a couple of great online resources:

https://www.psychologytoday.com/us/blog/the-heart-of-healing/202304/why-focusing-on-the-bottom-line-can-actually-hurt-profits

https://journals.sagepub.com/doi/abs/10.1177/0018726719858394

There is a *lot* of evidence and data to back up the assertions I've made in this section. All of that is on your side when attempting to convince a Bottom Liner of the error of their ways. Many of them don't intend to send the message that employees don't matter, so if you're feeling that way, make sure you tell them so. Don't let them excuse their behavior with statements like, "If we don't care about the bottom line, none of us will have jobs." That's a strawman argument. The issue isn't attention to the bottom line. It's attention to the bottom line *above all else* that is the problem. You can tell the Bottom Liner that you care about the bottom line too, which is why you're asking to be considered as important also, since your performance accounts for so much of it.

The Squirrel

Recall that Squirrels tend to move so quickly that they cause employees to feel like pylons on a raceway. Because so much of the negative impact of a Squirrel is unintended, Squirrel leaders are usually open to trying to change things once they become aware of the issues.

As I mentioned in Chapter 1, the most tragic cycle I see with Squirrel leaders is the Seagull Leadership pattern. Squirrels can move very quickly between topics and teams, and depending on the size of the organization, it can take some time before they swoop in to any given team. During that time, the team is working, creating, implementing, and innovating. It can feel euphoric and empowering until they realize that the Squirrel leader still has strong opinions about how things are done—often undoing the work the teams had been doing when that team's number comes up and they get the undivided, but brief, attention of the Squirrel leader. This leads to a cycle of the teams waiting for the next Squirrel visit to get approval on things before they move on. If Squirrels led relay race teams, they'd have batons on the ground everywhere.

How Do Squirrels Detoxify?

If you're a Squirrel leader, it sounds trite to just say that you need to slow down. That would be easy for me to suggest and it might be very difficult for you to implement. Most Squirrel leaders I've experienced would likely qualify as having ADHD. For reference, here are some of the symptoms of it:[48] [49]

- Carelessness and lack of attention to detail
- Continually starting new tasks before finishing old ones
- Poor organizational skills
- Inability to focus or prioritize
- Continually losing or misplacing things
- Forgetfulness
- Restlessness and edginess
- Difficulty keeping quiet, and speaking out of turn
- Blurting out responses and often interrupting others
- Inability to deal with stress
- Extreme impatience

    I'm not a psychologist and I'm not pretending to be one, but I do know that the way we show up at work is often similar to how we show up everywhere. If we snap at coworkers under stress, we probably snap at our partners or kids under stress also. So, it's reasonable to say that if you behave like a Squirrel—zooming from task to task leaving people with their mouths agape—there might be something physiological behind it. Unlike some of the other archetypes, who may be able to have a Scrooge-like perspective shift through a visceral experience, Squirrels may struggle to slow down with a brain that wants to quickly flutter from topic to topic.

    Adults who have ADHD often report that it feels like a superpower, and I certainly can see why. I'm often envious of their ability to hold so many topics in flight. But there is often a

---

[48] "Attention Deficit Hyperactivity Disorder (ADHD) Symptoms," National Health Services, last modified December 24, 2021, accessed December 7, 2023, https://www.nhs.uk/conditions/attention-deficit-hyperactivity-disorder-adhd/symptoms/.

[49] I'm specifically referring to ADHD rather than ADD. The H (Hyperactive) adds a component that I think is relevant for the Squirrel archetype. It's not just a hampered ability to focus, it's also a nuclear reactor's worth of energy to multitask and move at incredible speeds.

cost to others that is difficult for those with ADHD to notice. That cost is far more pronounced when the person with ADHD is in a position of leadership. So, if you know you're a Squirrel, consider asking people in other facets of your life if you show up similarly for them. Partners, kids, extended family, and friends are all great resources. If you see that the behaviors follow you everywhere in your life and are not seemingly in your control, consider getting tested for ADHD as a first step. Knowing if you have it could be a game changer for you in terms of coping strategies.

Managing Up to The Squirrel

If you report to a Squirrel, you will need to do a lot of reminding, recording, and reprioritizing. Some Squirrels are very good at remembering what they told you three weeks ago, and some are terrible at it but, universally, you can count on their instructions changing frequently. I find it helpful to maintain a list of priorities that are visible to yourself and the Squirrel. That way, when they come in and shift what you're working on with their typical "this is a top priority" flick of the wrist, you can say "Ok, if I make this my top priority, that means what used to be my number one is now number two and so on. Take a look at my list here. The impact to the timeline will be . . ." For most Squirrels, when they pass on an instruction, they quickly move it out of their minds. Those of us who are *following* that instruction know that it may involve days or weeks of work to complete. That is plenty of time for a Squirrel to reenter the picture and provide instructions that shift everything again.

To manage up, *you* must have the organizational skills and the focus you want *them* to have. If you are disorganized, you're doomed. To be very clear, you will need to *over own* the Squirrel's organization, as it relates to your work. This is for your own sanity. Just be careful not to shame the Squirrel. That will backfire on you. Instead, just be prepared with what instructions you're following and how the pursuit of any bright, shiny objects will impact the current course. Once they understand/remember/stop and think, they often back down from that bright, shiny object. If you don't want to be or can't be organized for a Squirrel leader, your only real option is to get away from them.

The other impact of working for a Squirrel is that they can micromanage very impulsively—fully engaged, then fully disengaged. This can be jarring and cause you to feel completely unempowered and disoriented. Make sure the Squirrel is aware of these impacts. Tell them that you're feeling more and more uncomfortable moving forward without them because they're often making changes to what you've done. Ask them what's holding them back from giving you more autonomy, emphasizing that it doesn't make sense for you to wait around for their input when they're always so busy.

The Graveyard Whistler

If your three hundred Spartans are facing a hundred thousand approaching enemies, your soldiers are looking for you to acknowledge the reality and instill confidence in themselves and you. "Yes, we're outnumbered. But we have far superior tactics, armor, and training. We are very prepared for this, and they don't know what's coming. For Sparta!"

Can you see the acknowledgment, the confidence, and the rallying cry there? Graveyard Whistlers (I'll refer to them as Whistlers for short) are missing the acknowledgment part. We don't want our leaders bathing in negativity like Eeyore from Winnie the Pooh, but acting as if there is no negativity is just as bad from an employee's perspective.

How Do Graveyard Whistlers Detoxify?

Recall that beliefs are a component of our mindsets and drive our actions. We only do what makes sense to us and honors our beliefs. Most Whistlers I know are in one of two camps of beliefs: They either believe that acknowledging negativity gives it power, or they believe that acknowledging it demoralizes employees and isn't a leader-like behavior because leaders are supposed to remain positive. Both of these beliefs are false for the same reason: They drive disconnection with employees, and disconnection is the *real* demotivator in these situations. This is especially true when a Whistler dismisses or ignores negativity being brought forward by the team itself. It is toxically positive for you to hand wave a challenge that the teams are bringing with a dismissive statement like, "How hard can it be? We got this."

As a Whistler, your first task is to identify and challenge any beliefs you have that ignoring or minimizing negativity is what leaders do. What leaders actually do is connect with those they lead. Connection creates followers, and followers create leaders. If your employees think you're oblivious or in denial they will be *less* inclined to follow you. Your credibility will suffer as well because they begin to wonder if you're delusional. What people want from their leaders is a comfort with discomfort. That creates safety for others to be real and shines spotlights on all the elephants in the room so they can be dealt with. If you are strongly resistant to embracing negativity, it may be worth exploring a bit of therapy as to why that may be the case. Again, I'm not arguing for you to swim in negativity and difficulty; I'm arguing for you to be able to acknowledge it, sit with it while others process it, and then lead them and yourself out of it. Some of the best leaders I've ever seen have found this balance. You can too.

Managing Up to a Graveyard Whistler

Most Whistlers have the best intentions. This is what makes it so hard to be led by them. On one hand, you may feel personally cared for and sheltered by a Whistler, but on the other hand your urge is not to follow them anywhere because they *seem to be* oblivious to what's really going on—even if they are, in fact, well aware of it. To manage up to a Whistler, you'll need to be explicit about what you need from them when it comes to dealing with negative topics. Say something like:

> I noticed that when I brought up the difficulties my team is having dealing with our unstable roadmap, you said that you know we can handle it. While I appreciate your confidence in us, it felt empty that

you moved so quickly past the problem. We were hoping for more acknowledgment from you of the problem and some curiosity about the details. Are you willing to do that?

Another example:

> During the all-hands meeting, several of us brought up that we're feeling overwhelmed, and you seemed to breeze past our comments. I know you really do care, but it felt like you didn't in that moment. Could we have a special meeting to discuss that topic more?

Being explicit with your Whistler leader is the best way for them to learn that their beliefs about avoiding negativity leading to better leadership outcomes are not true. The mistake employees of Whistlers make is not saying anything. This lets the Whistler conclude that their tactic was successful. You're not complaining so you must be a happy employee, and their leadership skills are the reason. Don't let them get away with avoiding facing issues head-on; help them face reality.

The Value of Coaching and Therapy

Whatever archetype you fit, there may be value in finding a good therapist *and* coach to help you through it. The difference between the two is typically therapists look backward in time to try to help you understand how your past has lent itself to your present. Coaches, meanwhile, are great for looking forward. Therapists are required to complete a lot of education and training and must hold a license to practice to lead you through your past. Coaches do not have that kind of training and are not qualified to help clients look backward. In fact, the coaching world has many imposters—and I say that as a coach myself (though to be clear, I'm a certified life and executive coach with over a thousand hours of training). Those of us who have been through the training can competently help our clients to reinvent themselves if that's what they want. But as it stands now, anyone can call themselves a coach, so you should check their credentials and get references.

Once you find a good coach, the most effective way to utilize them is to share what you're discovering with your therapist and work with your coach to implement improvements that you're working on. Coaches can challenge you to push your boundaries and grow. They can also hold you accountable. This is especially valuable when no one else feels like they have permission to do that in your life.

If you're serious about moving away from your toxic leadership archetypical behaviors, the most effective strategy is to use therapy to understand where it came from and coaching to learn how to fix it.

Part Four

Becoming a Better Company

Gall's Law: A complex system that works, most likely evolved from a simple system that worked. A complex system designed that way from scratch can never be made to work. You must start over with a simple working system.

– Dr. John Gall

In this final part of the book, we're going to look at two groups that contribute a great deal of root cause to toxic leadership and cultures inside most companies: human resources and finance.

Just like leaders don't wake up thinking, "How can I destroy this company today?" these groups aren't *trying* to create toxic cultures and environments. But regardless of their intentions, Senior HR and finance leaders often cultivate poor culture and incentivize toxic leadership by creating policies that accomplish their own goals but hamper the business on the frontline—often in ways that do not show up as a line item on the profit and loss statement.

Incentives

In 2023, the United Auto Workers union launched a strike against the big three American car manufacturers. I watched an interview with the CEO of General Motors, Mary Barra. It was pointed out in the interview that Ms. Barra has received a 34 percent raise over the past four years and makes approximately $29 million per year—or 365 times more than a typical auto worker. Why, the interviewer wanted to know, is it unreasonable for auto workers to also demand 34 percent increases? Ms. Barra defended her salary by noting that 92 percent of it is "performance based." That means that if she failed at "performance" and received none of that 92 percent, she would be left with a mere $2,320,000 per year (twenty-nine times more than a typical auto worker).

The more interesting facet of her answer lies in what she means by "performance." She means *stock performance*, not the performance of the company. And the truth is, the two are not connected in any predictable way. The stock market purports that shareholders are owners of a company when, in fact, they often behave more like renters. They want short-term gains even if it might mean future long-term losses. Most will jump ship the second the stock looks in danger of falling.

Because Ms. Barra is rewarded with stocks and then is bonused on the performance of that stock, she too is a shareholder who is incentivized to act like a renter. GM has laid off thousands of employees in recent years. They are behind Tesla in electric vehicle design and sales but spend billions of dollars each year buying back their shares. Each time they do so, the stock price goes up, increasing Barra's performance-based income.

Wall Street seems to like this behavior but is it a sign of a well-run company? I suppose that's debatable depending on what you think a healthy company looks like, but increasingly, stock performance doesn't track with decisions that contribute to the *long-term* success of a company or its employees, never mind society and the planet. The Milton Friedman theory that CEOs and other executives are first and foremost responsible for shareholder value (known as the Friedman Doctrine) has benefited shareholders while being devastating to just about everyone else. It gives those who run companies—who, again, *are also shareholders*—a free pass to choose the quickest, shortest path to decreased expenses and increased profits without regard for consumers, the planet, employee wellbeing, or society at large.

For our purposes here, most of the worst leadership behavior we see in companies stems directly from this doctrine and the policies and behaviors it spawns. It encourages sociopathic behavior in our companies and likely leads to sociopaths being promoted within them. I'm under no illusion that a company can truly change its behavior to caring more about employees, consumers, and the environment while its senior executives are financially rewarded *not to consider those things*. Publicly traded companies or those with those aspirations are under immense pressure to follow the formula: Treat employees, the planet, and society as cash machines to be exploited for profits.

Many human resources and finance policies are rooted in this formula to the detriment of everyone involved. Let's now examine each group to see how they contribute to negative outcomes without intending to and what they might do to turn things around.

DEEPER DIVE

The Infinite Game by Simon Sinek

Milton Friedman Was Wrong by Eric Posner: The Atlantic
https://www.theatlantic.com/ideas/archive/2019/08/milton-friedman-shareholder-wrong/596545/

Chapter 15: Human Resources

Fear-based management systems make good people lie. Fear doesn't make bad news go away; fear makes bad news go into hiding.

– Richard Sheridan, author of *Joy, Inc.: How We Built a Workplace People Love*

Building a place of work where talented people want to be is very much like developing a great product that customers want to buy.

– Natal Dank and Riina Hellström, authors of *Agile HR: Deliver Value in a Changing World of Work*

Human resources (HR) has two primary missions that seem to be at odds with one another at many companies. The first is to help the company attract, retain, and develop talent for the goals it is trying to achieve. The second is to protect the company from lawsuits from that very workforce through the creation and enforcement of policy.

The conflict of these goals is written all over the faces of the professionals in the HR profession. I meet many of them at leadership retreats and other coach training. They are usually deeply empathetic, talented, and caring people who want to help the company grow and to help employees find fulfillment in their work. They correctly view that as a win-win.

Instead of being able to do this work, however, they often find themselves acting more like hired guns whose primary goal is to keep the company out of court—even if it means siding with terrible leadership behavior and behaving deceitfully. HR must do this under the guise of representing the employees' best interest when, in fact, the employees are often completely unrepresented in these matters. I had one HR professional describe her role as leaving her feeling "icky" most days. She clearly disliked her role as a representative of Goliath against David.

This split personality has not gone unnoticed by the workforce. Increasingly, HR is viewed more like an untrusted spy for the company rather than someone really interested in employee growth and support. At many companies, HR *promotes itself* as the latter quite deceptively, which only adds to the distrust. Talking to HR about a poor leader at the company is like discussing tax reduction strategies with an IRS auditor. Sure, IRS auditors are experts in tax law, they just aren't motivated to help you in the way you may be hoping. The true motives of HR at most companies reinforce the "us versus them" vibe that employees often have with the company and its leaders. Much of the good work that HR does for employees with benefits packages, hiring bonuses, and retention strategies is often overshadowed by this legal enforcement role.

Reimagining Human Resources

What would it look like if HR were to shed their enforcement, lawyerly duties and send them over to (and under) the legal department at the company? Doing so would sharpen the line between recruitment/development and termination. And wouldn't everyone involved like that line to be sharper anyway? There's nothing worse than getting put on a Performance Improvement Plan (PIP) and not knowing whether that plan is genuinely there to help you improve or if you're really in a no-win situation and should probably begin looking for a new job. What a waste of a great tool to coach an employee with! And if the purpose is really to manage the employee out, why not just bite the bullet and tell the employee that? Offer them job search help and a nice severance package including some paid healthcare. PIPs take a lot of time and energy from HR, leaders, and employees. I would argue that this time costs more than a good severance package would—especially when those severance packages are often still offered at the end of the PIP process.

If PIPs are being used to cover the legal ass of the company but are not genuinely being used to correct a behavior or coach real improvement, then they're nothing but expensive code for, "You're fired . . . just in slow motion." That's a waste of everyone's time. Many of the dysfunctional teams I work with who have a brilliant asshole on them use PIPS in this way for two reasons:

1. There is no official way to get this employee the coaching they need to improve that isn't cloaked in the idea that their job is basically over.

2. The process to fire them when they are unable/unwilling to change their approach is so burdensome that some leaders simply don't have the bandwidth to do it.

When the line gets sharper between coaching and parting ways, we can let the HR that is free of that enforcement work focus on the work that HR specialists really signed up for:

attracting, retaining, and coaching employees. I like to refer to this new, more focused department as human development (HD).

When we've moved the termination activities under the legal department and the recruitment/development duties under human development, the explicit agreement we make with employees is that HD is *never* involved with termination or removal. They may use PIPs but only in the service of clearly helping employees grow, never as scarlet letters or an encoded way of telling employees to take a hike. You can work with HD voluntarily any time you want to grow as a human, or someone can ask—even assign—you to get help from them but, when you are working with Human Development, you will know that you aren't in trouble, you're learning. This is the growth mindset manifested in organizational policy and design.

If it ever begins to look like it's not going to work out at the company, you ideally arrive at that conclusion *with* your HD representative. Depending on the situation, they may help you find a different job at the company or find one at a different company. When the latter happens, only then do you cross over to the "part ways" path and begin speaking with a specialist in legal who prepares your parting documents. Obviously, blatant violations of policy or law would put someone directly into that legal loop, but so many tragic scenarios play out at companies where well-intentioned employees either make a mistake or are trying to do the right thing for the company and are maneuvered directly into the parting ways category instead of the development one.

HD should offer a full training program where they teach leadership and other important skills that every employee needs to work together better. They also should offer leadership coaching to *all leaders* and not just the senior leaders as most do now. All leaders need help to become better leaders, and they need on-the-ground support for that work, not just class time.

A human development group is also involved with exit interviews. They may even run that practice. Their job during this process is to build trust, ask powerful questions, and try to get to the root of the reason people are leaving. If patterns emerge (say, everyone who leaves is complaining about a certain leader), then the immediate action is to bring that leader in for coaching. If that leader turns out to have toxic tendencies that they won't let go of despite coaching, they can enter the parting ways pathway. Human development should see it as one of their core jobs to keep a diligent watch for drops of poison in leadership roles. They should compile monthly reports for executive leadership outlining turnover, exit interview trends, social media ratings, and other important data related to employee engagement and retention.

Of course, exit interviews generate trailing indicators of problems. To get a leading indicator, HD should also administer and process regular engagement surveys. These should be able to be completed in less than thirty minutes and be given at least quarterly. They should be anonymous at the individual level but coded so that team, leadership, and structure can be determined. That way low engagement scores can be traced back to the leaders accountable. Again, this isn't to get anyone in trouble. It's to figure out where coaching and training are needed.

New policies to meet recruitment, retention, development, and engagement targets should be focus-group centered with leaders from all levels coming together to understand the problem and work on the policies together. There should also be regular check-ins to discuss how things are going and course correct as needed.

HD may not have the authority to fix all issues revealed by the processes they administer, but with an executive team committed to employee engagement, they can safely provide the data those leaders need to make the right decisions.

Are there scenarios that fall between the cases I've made here? Yes. And I'm not pretending that I've got some magic bullet idea here. Some of these things are currently done in HR at some companies; however, these activities are undermined by a complete lack of trust from employees because of the split personality and deceitful stance so many HR groups are forced to operate under because of their assigned objectives. Remember the mantra I keep repeating: Credibility is a multiplier. Human resources, as it's practiced today at most companies, operates in a credibility vacuum. They get around it by using authoritarian tactics, but that doesn't change hearts and minds and it won't increase any Glassdoor scores either.

Disconnection from Policy Impact

HR's goals are simple to write down and are quite numeric: "Increase percentage of minority groups at the company by 10 percent. Increase number of women in leadership roles by 15 percent." These are great goals! But too often HR creates policies that aim to accomplish them without a closed-loop connection to the impact of those policies at the frontline. There is a "We've made a decision, you work it out" vibe towards frontline leaders. At the policy decision level, it's a simple problem to describe. At the execution level, it's often quite a bit more complex and HR is rarely aware of, connected to, or concerned with that complexity.

As an example, I once worked with a company that hired a lot of contractors—a practice that has become much more common in the past decade or so. Because of reasons that I still do not completely understand, HR said that these workers could not work this way for more than a year (2,080 hours). At that point, managers were told that they either must hire the person or end the contract. It was called being "2080'd." As you can imagine, by the end of that year, these folks knew their jobs well and, if they were good at them, were often quite popular with their teammates. They may have even become subject matter experts for very specific systems at the company. As such, the leaders of these teams wanted to convert these contractors into full-time employees (FTEs) at this stage.

It seems so simple, but at this company, it was not. The first challenge these leaders encountered was getting approval from finance to hire an FTE for the team (see next chapter). If this 2080 moment happened to occur during a hiring freeze, there would be no new hires or conversions. This would create a flat-out loss for the team as perhaps one of their key people had to leave without a backfill.

Even if the full-time role were to be approved by finance, there were additional hurdles to jump at this company. HR had another policy that any contractor wishing to convert to full-time would have to interview for the role—competing with both outside and inside candidates. This policy was an effort to increase the mobility of internal employees, make sure the company was hiring the best talent, and, according to an HR rep I spoke with, "make the whole process fairer." These are noble goals that I support, but the policy had some chilling and wide-reaching impacts on the organization:

- **Contractors would leave before they could be converted.** Contractors nearing the end of their contract didn't want to chance not getting past the interview because another candidate interviewed well, so they often would seek and accept new job offers at other companies before their 2080 moment. After all, people need to feed themselves and their families.
- **Contractors felt misled and manipulated.** Contractors viewed themselves as being on a yearlong job interview for that full-time job. In fact, many were assured that there was a job waiting for them if they performed well. So, this interview process was seen as a slap in the face and an act of bad faith from the company. Not to mention they would be competing against people who would not need to spend that year as a contractor since any outside candidate would be brought in as an FTE right from the start. If this was "fairer," then whom was it fairer for?
- **The grass is always greener.** You can nearly *always* find someone who at least looks better on paper if you look. Some people interview well and turn out not to be all that great. Some talented people freeze up during interviews. This policy sometimes resulted in letting someone go who was doing the job well only to be replaced by someone (who would now be an FTE) who turned out not to be as good of a fit or who lacked the

skills the contractor had.
- **The team wasted time.** The team members and leader had to spend significant amounts of time and energy to interview candidates—some of whom didn't stand a chance when the team really liked their current teammate. This wasted the candidates' time as well.

I wanted to go through this example in detail because it illustrates the disconnection between policy intention and reality. These kinds of impacts can happen with most policies, but with HR policies there is often no feedback loop in place to discover them. No collaboration with frontline leaders to see what concerns they have. No chance to see if the policy is having the intended impact or if unforeseen negative outcomes are occurring.

Contractors: A Class System

There's another problem in the above example. Did you spot it? The contractor relationship is really a class system inside of corporate America. FTEs are higher-class citizens than contractors. In many companies, they even get different badge colors. This results in the formation of insiders and outsiders within the company's workforce that benefit *no one*.

We've already talked about how employees are often treated as expendable units to be trimmed at the first sign of lower profits. Well, contractors are even *more* expendable. The expendability of contractors is built into the contractor relationship as a feature, not a bug. A contractor is considered self-employed and therefore companies they work *with* (not for) are customers of theirs, and the relationship can usually be severed by either side for any reason. But this system is being abused by companies, who gain many financial and legal benefits from hiring contractors instead of full-time employees. Here are a few:

- Increased flexibility to easily scale the workforce up or down.
- Ability to reduce their workforce without needing to give

advance notice to contractors, state and local governments, or Wall Street.
- Reduced or eliminated training and equipment costs.
- No employee benefits. No healthcare, stock options, profit sharing, or worker's compensation. No paid vacation or sick time.

I hope you're spotting that all these benefits to the company are risks or downsides to the contractor. To be clear, there are people who want to work for themselves, have the freedom to have multiple clients, and perhaps unlock a wage ceiling that exists when working as a full-time employee of a company by doing contract work. Perhaps they get medical insurance from a spouses' job or are willing to pay for it on their own. For these people, willingly entering this type of relationship with a company is usually a net positive. But increasingly, companies are advertising most of their job openings as "contract to hire" rather than FTE. This is forcing unemployed workers to unwillingly assume these risks and downsides if they want to feed themselves and their families.

More to the point of leadership impacts, the single largest effect of this trend on team and company performance is that teams never achieve synergy. As a team and leadership performance coach, I often begin my work with one-on-one meetings with each team member. I ask a lot of powerful questions to try to elicit what's going on with the team. When that team is loaded with contractors, they will parade through my meeting room one at a time, each telling me how amazing things are and how they just can't think of a single thing they'd change about the place. Then the single FTE on the team enters the room, closes the door, and says, "Please help us. We're a mess."

The fact that the team is loaded with contractors means they are all reaching their 2080 moments in a staggered fashion all year long. And because the company sees these people as numbers, they won't convert them and instead force the team to lose a teammate and onboard another, causing everyone to slow down. There is virtually no institutional knowledge and no trust on the team among members because no one feels safe to say anything negative. All of this is occurring well outside the eyes of the leaders in finance and HR who are responsible for these hiring policies. But the cost of labor number sure looks great on the financial reports, I guess.

An Opportunity for Human Resources

Human resources, as it is practiced today, is missing an immense opportunity to represent employees' voices back to the leadership team and to advocate for employees in matters that affect them. A properly implemented HR group would not only have the responsibility but also the authority to force their peers in leadership to explore and exhaust all other options before simply laying employees off or chopping benefits. It would help the company develop leaders and keep the company values front and center during all discussions. It would cocreate policies with frontline leaders to accomplish company goals and outcomes while honoring those values. Finally, it would make sure that leaders are continuously reminded that those they lead are human beings with goals, dreams, and families—not headcount, human capital, or resources.

DEEPER DIVE

Agile HR: Deliver Value in a Changing World of Work by Natal Dank and Riina Hellström

---

CHAPTER 16: FINANCE

Once, after giving a speech at an Air Force base, I asked the colonel in charge, "I'm just curious. How do you teach these young men and women to kill people?" He thought for a minute and said, "Well, we don't teach them to kill people; we teach them to take out targets that made bad decisions." I said, "Well, I'll be darned. We do the same thing in business. We call it downsizing or layoffs. We don't say we're destroying the lives of fifteen people today."

— Bob Chapman

Before we get too deeply into this chapter, if you're in finance at your company I'm going to just pause here and strongly recommend that you read the three books below:

> **DEEPER DIVE**
>
> *Beyond Budgeting* by Jeremy Hope and Robin Fraser
>
> *Implementing Beyond Budgeting* by Bjarte Bogsnes
>
> *Our Least Important Asset: Why the Relentless Focus on Finance and Accounting is Bad for Business and Employees* by Peter Cappelli

These three books make strong in-depth arguments for why and how companies need to change the way they think about money and finance if they want to transform to a people-first company. In-depth arguments about this are outside the scope of this book but are handled respectfully and realistically in these deeper dive books. In this chapter, I'm just going to point out some glaring faults with the way we do things now. For many employees at companies—even employees in relatively high-up leadership positions—there is no chance to stand up against a finance policy that is causing unintended negative impacts. Finance is treated as an untouchable final word. "The protectors of shareholder value hath spoken and they've commanded the following . . ."

The Distant King

Most employees—as I mentioned, even leaders—have a distant and tangential relationship with finance. Many quality-of-life aspects of work seem rooted in the policies and decisions made by some mysterious person in finance:

- Struggling with your workload because someone quit but can't be backfilled? Blame finance.
- Can't hire a full-time employee but can hire a temporary

worker for a year? Blame finance.
- Can't expense the lunch you just paid for with a vendor? finance's fault.
- Can't give an employee a retention pay increase but can hire their replacement for the same or more money than the original employee was asking for? Probably finance.
- Can't travel to be face-to-face with teammates or clients? finance.
- Being asked to predict your future needs six or twelve months from now in a volatile market? Almost certainly finance.
- Told to cut 5 percent of your staff this quarter despite record profits and increasing workload on your team? finance again.

Like HR policies, finance policies have a lot of unintended negative consequences at the frontline of most companies. Brené Brown uses the phrase "invisible army" to describe the way people get others to back down. "Customers are asking . . ." Which customers? "People are saying . . ." Which people? Finance is an invisible army at most companies. "I'm sorry you'll need to lay off 5 percent of your staff. It's come down from finance."

    Not to beat up on the individuals in finance, but the department itself is probably the closest you can get to simulating a king ruling a kingdom, except in this case the king never comes out of the castle and never sees his people. Most people never see the CFO or hear from them directly, but their work lives are deeply impacted by them.

    There seems to be only one group of people that a CFO seems to be beholden to and that's shareholders. Shareholders are the invisible army of renter-owners that the CFO uses to get others to back down. "I know this is tough, but shareholders are served best by this decision."

    It bears repeating that much of this shareholder value stuff is self-serving for most senior executives, who often hold massive numbers of shares in the company. If the share value goes up, so too does the portfolio value of these leaders. In an ideal world, doing right by the employees, customers, and the planet would lead to a higher share price. But we don't live in an ideal world. Finance and the Generally Accepted Accounting Principles (GAAP) they follow often incentivize policy decisions that are unhealthy for the company and its employees. As Peter Cappelli points out in his Harvard Business Review Article entitled "How Financial Accounting Screws Up HR"*[50]*:

> Firms skimp on training and development [...] and tightly limit head count even when they're understaffed. They increasingly move work to nonemployees, like leased workers, and replace pensions with more-expensive 401(k) plans. They do such counterproductive things because U.S. financial reporting standards treat employees and investments in them as expenses or liabilities, which make companies look less valuable to investors.

Essentially, Cappelli is arguing that many of the long-term unhealthy hiring and operating policies that companies adopt stem from GAAP. It seems so anticlimactic to say that all this heartache, poor treatment, and lack of concern for employees boils down to . . . accounting practices. Is it really surprising though? Put a system in place—any system—and human beings will learn to game it. GAAP is a system like any other and it is being gamed. What I'm here to say is that this manipulation is a real self-own[51] or, if you're a sports fan, own goal. When companies play these games to make their books look better, they think they're just moving numbers around. But the impacts to engagement, turnover, performance, and innovation are significant and insidiously lagging. As Cappelli argues, it may be time to revisit what is generally accepted about these accounting principles.

---

[50] Peter Cappelli, "How Financial Accounting Screws Up HR," *Harvard Business Review*, last modified February 2023, accessed September 26, 2023, https://hbr.org/2023/01/how-financial-accounting-screws-up-hr.

[51] As with many slang terms, sometimes a single phrase can capture a real human experience. Self-own comes from the gaming culture and it defines when someone's actions harm themselves while they're trying to help themselves.

The Disconnection from Humanity

As I mentioned earlier, leadership is a lot easier when you can relieve yourself of any concern that actual human beings are being impacted by your decisions. I suspect this is why the king doesn't come down from the castle too often. Best not to have to look those in the face who you just argued to have laid off so their jobs can be moved to a staffing agency.

In popular culture, we try to teach about the perils of this kind of behavior in *A Christmas Carol*, first published in 1843 (yes, we've been dealing with money-fixated executives for literally centuries). One doesn't need to wonder what would have happened to Tiny Tim had Scrooge not been forced to witness the past, present, and future with his own eyes. It's a shame that the takeaway from that story for many modern executives appears to be to avoid looking in the first place.

One decision to layoff or outsource. One cell on a large spreadsheet. Hundreds or even thousands of lives affected. Spouses may need to quit their jobs because the laid off employee can only find work in another state. Kids from those families may need to change schools. Friendships will fade. People with medical issues will suddenly face the reality of not having health insurance *or* income. Sometimes arguments and fighting take place and families are torn apart altogether.

Leaders of all levels at the company will utter some form of the phrase "It's out of my hands. The decision was made. You'll have to figure out how to make it work." In other words, "We made a decision that deeply impacts you without consulting you. Whatever ideas you had to help us achieve these goals are unwelcome at this point. Be a good soldier and follow orders."

Until we get regrounded in the idea that humans are what make companies successful and direct finance to adjust its priorities, senior leaders will continue struggling with the many concepts I've outlined in this book, resulting in toxic leadership that will slowly and painfully destroy our companies—especially our publicly traded ones.

Chapter 17: Saving Starfish

I worry that business leaders are more interested in material gain than they are in having the patience to build up a strong organization, and a strong organization starts with caring for their people.

— John Wooden, American basketball coach and player

100 percent of employees are people. 100 percent of customers are people. 100 percent of investors are people. If you don't understand people, you don't understand business.

— Simon Sinek

The best advice Quincy Jones ever gave me was don't be cool, be warm. There are a lot of people in the world trying to be cool. What we need is more warm people.

— Jacob Collier, Grammy Award-winning musician and songwriter

While writing this book, I had a crisis of faith, of sorts. Despite my overall cynicism for the way things are naturally incentivized to evolve in a capitalist world—especially one as unregulated as the one we find ourselves in now—it might surprise you to know that I'm quite an optimist about the future of leadership. I believe that human beings are acting this way out of ignorance rather than malice. I'm not a religious man but Jesus's statement in Luke 23:24 rings through my mind. "Father, forgive them; for they know not what they do." Inherent in that is a belief that if people just learned more, they'd do better. It is that belief that pushed me to write the book you're now nearly finished reading.

Several months ago, however, that belief all came crashing down for me.

First a little background. I had just wrapped up a short engagement with a leader at a large company. My assignment with her was not to coach her on being a leader, it was to help her integrate with a team she had just been assigned to lead. While this leader, let's call her Linda, seemed to have good intentions, I spotted very quickly that something was amiss but I couldn't quite put my finger on what it was.

As part of this assignment, I interviewed Linda's new team. One of the interviewees, who had worked for Linda previously, told me that Linda had a big run-in with one of her employees several months back. The person she got into a battle with was her senior engineer, a subject matter expert. Something Linda was asking the team to do was a very bad idea, according to this engineer, and he fought hard against it. Eventually Linda relented but not in a healthy way. She disengaged from the team, and they rarely saw her again. She stopped showing up at the team's meetings.

To say that I had an entire field of red flags waving in my mind would be an understatement—but again, my job here was not to coach Linda. She had already received a great deal of coaching from others. So, I had to work with what I had.

I fulfilled my assignment with Linda and moved on to the next: coaching a newly promoted leader we'll call Jim, in this same company. I had immediately pegged him as a fantastic leader. I can spot them very quickly. Good leaders may not always know *what* to do, but they always know *why* they're doing it—for those they lead. Jim was very clearly centered on his employees.

I had only had two sessions with Jim before I was informed that he would no longer be working with me because he had been laid off. The company decided that any employee who got a "needs improvement" in the previous year would be a candidate for being laid off. Jim met that criterion.

It turns out, Jim was that senior engineer of Linda's, and you guessed it, Linda gave him a "needs improvement" because of their disagreement.

I just stared at the ceiling in disbelief, having just witnessed yet another example—in a long line of examples—of a company that appeared to have a knack for laying off their best leaders while retaining their worst. When I see this occur, it affects me in a deep way. Like watching the hero in a movie be slaughtered. You almost can't believe your own eyes. *This can't be happening! I hate this movie!*

Watching Jim get laid off and learning that it was Linda's assessment of him that made it happen was like irony poisoning. I stared at the flashing cursor that would need to transform into the remaining chapters of this book and thought, *Why am I doing this? I can't save these companies from themselves. It's hopeless. The incentives are all wrong and way too strong for me to hope that I can entice companies to change their behaviors.* I almost just stopped writing and gave up. But, as I have during similar crucial crossroads in my life, I decided to call my friend and coach, Pat Goonan.

Pat always has a way of dropping wisdom into my world. He is wicked smart with a very good memory. He speaks cryptically sometimes, telling you exactly what you need to hear even if it doesn't make immediate sense. What kind of guru would he be if he did it any other way?

That day, Pat listened to me talk about my crisis of faith in essentially my own ability to make an impact on the problem of toxic leadership. He told me a story that I later learned was adapted from a book by Loren C. Eiseley and Wystan Hugh Auden called *The Star Thrower*[52] that goes like this:

> A young girl was walking along a beach upon which thousands of starfish had been washed up during a terrible storm. When she came to each starfish, she would pick it up, and throw it back into the ocean. People watched her with amusement.
>
> She had been doing this for some time when a man approached her and said, "Little girl, why are you doing this? Look at this beach! You can't save all these starfish. You can't begin to make a difference!"
>
> The girl seemed crushed, suddenly deflated. But after a few moments, she bent down, picked up another starfish, and hurled it as far as she could into the ocean. Then she looked up at the man and replied, "Well, I made a difference for that one!"
>
> The old man looked at the girl inquisitively and thought about what she had said and done. Inspired, he joined the little girl in throwing starfish back into the sea. Soon others joined, and all the starfish were saved.

Pat's message was clear. Focus on one leader at a time, not one company at a time. The new leader you help today will improve the lives of everyone who works for them, and they could be the CEO of their own company tomorrow, impacting even more people. We make a difference one starfish at a time. If you've made it this far, I hope you are one of those starfish.

As we conclude this journey through toxic leadership, one thing should be abundantly clear by now: Toxic leaders are toxic because of their seeming indifference, either intentional or accidental, to the humans they lead. In some way or another, toxic leaders are so self-focused they've lost the difference between managing and leading. They're so organization-focused they are missing the fact that the organization is nothing without its people. Like the ghosts of Christmas past, present, and future, hundreds of authors have written thousands of books for decades trying to explain the antidote to toxic leadership: caring about

---

[52] Loren C. Eiseley and Wystan Hugh Auden, The Star Thrower (Orlando [etc.]: Harcourt, 1979), 169.

the people we lead at least as much as the profits we're trying to make from their labor.

The best leaders I've ever met and worked with were not walking around with master's degrees in leadership. They weren't handed down magical knowledge of leadership from a scholar at an Ivy League school. They do one simple thing consistently day after day. They ask themselves, "What is the best decision for my people?" They know that if they consistently do the best they can for their people, those people will always rise to return the favor, and that always benefits the company. Time and time again, I've watched this formula work. I've seen people give companies their all because they knew their leader cared about them. It's not magic but it sure feels magical when it's happening.

As a company consultant who specializes in helping companies turn around employee engagement and increase performance, I've learned that getting those results requires a number of steps. None of them is more important than leaders at all levels courageously searching for ways for their companies to get the outcomes they need while caring for employees, their families, society, and the planet. Yes, it is significantly more challenging to lead this way than it is to care only about profit, but it's not impossible. I'm reminded of a quote from American writer and civil rights activist James Baldwin: "Not everything that is faced can be changed, but nothing can be changed until it is faced."

Are you up for it? Do you feel the nearly overwhelming responsibility of it? Good. Leadership is a responsibility, not a reward. The world needs your caring leadership more than ever now. I make a difference. You make a difference. Through our work and the work of other great leaders who all decide to pick up a starfish and throw it as far as we can back into the water, we will detoxify our workplaces . . . removing one drop of poison at a time.

APPENDIX A

YOUR MINDSET ABOUT LEADERSHIP

Using the following definitions, complete the form on the next page to break down your mindset about leadership.

- **Beliefs**: Something you believe but cannot or have not attempted to prove (e.g., "People work better under a deadline.").
- **Values**: Something you value more than something else—even if you leave the something else off the statement (e.g., "I value honesty," "I value loyalty"). If you want some help coming up with your values, consider visiting this website for help: https://scottjeffrey.com/personal-core-values/
- **Principles**: A strong conclusion that honors beliefs and values. These can sometimes come from hard lessons (betrayal, epiphanies, life changing moments). Usually completing the sentence, "As a leader, I strive to always/never . . ." will help you find principles.
- **Processes**: These are behaviors we have and patterns we follow that we've put in place to help us honor and reinforce our values, beliefs, and principles.

Mindset Exercise

Beliefs

I have the following beliefs that are related to being a good leader:

1. _____
2. _____
3. _____

Values

I have the following values that are related to being a good leader:

1. _____
2. _____
3. _____

Principles

I have formed the following principles related to being a good leader. As a leader, I strive to [always/never]:

1. _____
2. _____
3. _____

Behaviors/Processes

List some behaviors or processes you have put in place that reinforce your beliefs, values, and principles above:

1. _____
2. _____
3. _____

APPENDIX B

THE TWENTY-FIRST CENTURY LEADERSHIP MANIFESTO

Business is facing a crisis in employee engagement. Loyalty is low; turnover is high. Employees are disconnecting from their work. Many business consulting firms seem to be about teaching leaders how create a vision and to speak to the crisis they're facing with employees. But we're not in this crisis because leaders are *saying* the wrong things. We're in it because they're *doing* the wrong things.

Employees are so disengaged they are no longer listening. Many don't even show up at all-hands meetings to hear the messages anymore because leadership credibility is at an all-time low. Intentional or not, actions are not lining up with words. Are you ready to try something different? There is no time to waste with more talk. We must do. If you are ready to do something, begin by adopting these five tenets as core beliefs at your company:

Joy Rolls Uphill

Employees come first. Before shareholder value. Before customers. Happy employees stay longer, are intrinsically motivated, and innovate better products and services; better products and services make happy customers; and happy customers increase our bottom line.

Loyalty Bounces Up

Loyalty cannot be commanded or bought. It bounces back at us when we send it downward through our organizations. If it's not bouncing back at us, we're doing something wrong.

Credibility Is a Multiplier

Credibility comes from saying what we'll do, then doing it. Over and over. When we have it, we don't waste any time convincing those we lead. When we don't, our words don't move anyone or anything. Earning and protecting credibility is the foundation of twenty-first century leadership and the beginning of a trusting relationship between our employees and the company's leaders.

Employees Are Human Beings

We will not make the right decisions affecting employees if we use euphemisms that abstract us from their humanity. They're not resources, headcount, or capital. They're people.

A Healthy Society Begins at Work

Employees' home lives are directly and significantly impacted by the large portion of their lives spent at work. Happy, healthy, fairly paid, fulfilled employees show up as better citizens, partners, spouses, family members, and parents, which benefits all of society for decades beyond today. This isn't merely correlation, it's causation.

You can find a copy of this manifesto along with the complete list of Deeper Dive recommendations at motivatedoutcomes.com. Remember to visit our YouTube Channel called Motivated Outcomes for hot takes on leadership and team performance topics.

Printed in the USA
CPSIA information can be obtained
at www.ICGtesting.com
JSHW010828260324
59910JS00007B/58/J